Skills & Tactics of GOLF

Skills & Tactics of GOLF

Marshall Cavendish
London & Sydney

Designed by Bryan Austin Associates

Published by Marshall Cavendish Books Limited
58 Old Compton Street
London W1V 5PA

© Marshall Cavendish Limited 1980

First printing 1980

Printed in Hong Kong

ISBN (hardback edition) 0 85685 821 8
ISBN (paperback edition) 0 85685 824 2

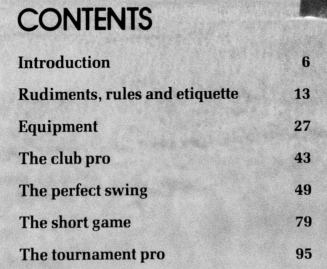

CONTENTS

INTRODUCTION

There is some doubt about where exactly the game of golf started. Some claim that the earliest version originated in Holland where, as early as the thirteenth century, people were hitting a ball with a club – mainly across ice. Others insist that it began on a Scottish hillside near Gullane on the east coast, when a young shepherd used his crook to hit stones, and by playing from 'pyre' to 'pyre' actually built a golf course. At the time, of course, there was quite a shipping trade between these countries so perhaps there is some link. However, although there is doubt about the origin, there is no question that it was the Scots who developed the game and indeed took it around the world. It is from their version that the golf swing developed.

The equipment available at that time created the shape and style of the golf swing and as it became more sophisticated, so the swing changed. When the golf ball was first made of a leather cover wrapped around an unknown filling (later, in the sixteenth century balls were stuffed with tightly packed feathers), it meant that the heads of the clubs needed to be made of wood and attached to longer shafts for the ball to be "swept" into flight. This was the beginning of the flatter arc which has been associated with the Scottish swing for generations, the timing of which required a lateral body movement known as swaying (which is avoided today).

In this century great strides have been made and golf equipment has undergone major changes. Indeed, in the past 50 years the swing has had to change dramatically

Right: The famous print of the Captain of the Society of Golfers at Blackheath, 1778. Royal Blackheath is the oldest golf club in England.

Below: A golf match on the links of St Andrews in 1798, with the clubhouse, now the traditional home of golf, in the background.

TO THE SOCIETY OF GOFFERS AT BLACKHEATH.

This Plate is with just Respect Dedicated by Their most humble Servant.

Samuel Francis Abbott.

'By the Lord Harry, this shall not go for nothing' — Cock O' the Green.

Bobby Locke, four-times winner of the British Open.

Above: Ben Hogan, three times winner of the US Open.

Opposite: Jasper National Park Golf Course, Alberta, Canada.

with the introduction and advancement of the steel-shafted club and the rubber-cored ball, and a much more central movement has evolved, with a simpler relationship between arms, wrists and hands. Whereas the old clubhead was very long and bound to the end of the long, whippy, wooden shaft, and had to operate like a fan, opening and closing, the modern club, with its short head, through which the firm steel-tube shaft passes, demands a simple, more direct movement. The ball, which is now constructed of strands of rubber wound around a central core and covered by a specially dimpled shell, gives immediate backspin when struck and does not require the "sweeping" its predecessors did.

The past 100 years has also seen a rapid progression in the ranks of those players called professionals, from being simply the best caddy who was then given a little wooden hut from which he might oversee the other caddies and, at the same time, repair and even make clubs for the golfers who played on the course, to the modern professional. When one sees the privately built course and residential village named Muirfield Village in Ohio, entirely paid for by Jack Nicklaus's personal millions and named after Muirfield in Scotland (next door to Gullane, home of the shepherd boy) where Jack won his first championship, and then reads the quotation of the captain of Muirfield, written exactly 100 years ago, explaining that Muirfield as a **links** was 'a piece of wasteland which exists between the beach and the mainland, on which a few geese, rabbits, and golf professionals might scrape a meagre living', the progress speaks for itself. There are, in fact, two distinct types of professionals: the tournament player, who makes his living by travelling the world playing for prize money; and the club professional, who remains attached to a club and looks after the golfing requirements of its members, teaching them to play and selling them equipment. Both are housed under the banner of the Professional Golfers' Association (PGA), but serve separate divisions.

Golf courses have changed dramatically from the days when the links were strips of land, cropped close by sheep and cattle, and on which sand dunes were the original bunkers. Today, many courses have man-made layouts. In the early days of golf, or *gouf* as it was then called, the game was played over whatever number of holes could be fitted into the land available. Even the traditional home of golf, St Andrews, in Scotland, had only a large enough strip of land for ten holes to be played on it out along the coast. However, one day, someone decided to play back to the town using the same greens, hence today's great course with its huge double greens, some as large as a soccer pitch, played

once on the way out and once again on the way back. So, the narrow strips of linksland brought about the expression of **outward** and **inward** halves, with the first leaving the town and the second returning to it, and eighteen holes became the accepted norm for the game.

Golf courses are now, with the aid of modern equipment and irrigation, constructed in areas which used to be deserts, like Las Vegas; in rugged mountain forests like Banff Springs in Canada; in the former paddy fields of Penina in Portugal; and on land which seemed fit only for goats in the case of the beautiful Torrequebrada, home of the 1979 Spanish Open Championship.

Early golf matches took the form of **match play**, where there was a direct challenge, with a hole-by-hole result between two players or two pairs. In those days the ball was played from wherever it came to rest and clubs were specially designed to extricate balls from gulleys, cart ruts, or any other hazard. As the game grew, **medal play** or **stroke play** was introduced where many players could compete against each other over the same course by keeping a record of all strokes taken over the whole round. Today, major events are played over four rounds (72 holes) with very large numbers of competitors. Indeed, in many open championships there have to be qualifying events played to eliminate hundreds in the **cut** prior to the final stages. A standard set of rules exists and a player is now normally allowed to drop clear of many of the obstacles which used to be accepted as 'a rub of the green'. Even if not allowed to do so without penalty, he can certainly do so, at his own discretion, by adding a penalty stroke. With the elimination of those dreadful hazards, many of the irons which had been designed to cope with difficult situations became illegal, and the modern-day set, with many stringent specifications set out by the Royal and Ancient Club at St Andrews, golf's ruling body, now consists of a maximum of fourteen clubs.

From this long history a very high standard of good sportsmanship and fellowship has evolved, both at amateur and professional level. It is a pleasure to be involved with the game, as well, of course, to play it to one's full potential. This book is designed to guide its readers through the common-sense rules, laying great stress on etiquette, which goes hand in hand. From generations of tournament professionals has been learned a method of swinging the club and a mental approach to positive scoring which has been adopted and adapted to suit golfers of all standards, on all types of courses and in all conditions. Readers may learn the descriptive language which the golf teacher uses and so benefit, either when receiving tuition or indeed when building a swing on their own.

Roberto de Vicenzo of the Argentine. Winner of no fewer than 39 national championships.

Henry Cotton of Great Britain, British Open Champion 1934-37-48.

Above: Jack Nicklaus, three times winner of the US and British Open Championships.
Opposite: The famous Valley of Sin in front of the 18th green at St Andrews.

CHAPTER 1

RUDIMENTS, RULES AND ETIQUETTE

The rules of golf have evolved to cover every aspect of the game – from how the par for the course is determined to the penalties involved in running foul of the hazards of the course.

The rules of golf are set, in Britain, by the Royal and Ancient Club at St Andrews, and, in the United States, by the United States Golf Association. There are, however, additional local rules set by individual clubs.

The golf course

Golf is played as an 18-hole game divided into two halves of nine holes each. In the case of nine-hole courses the holes are played twice, often using different teeing areas for variation. The halves are known as the outward and inward nines – although modern golf courses give no impression of going out or coming in from anywhere, and in fact often, when space is limited, resemble a maze. Nevertheless, the description of halves came when the strip of linksland was the home of the golf course and being so narrow meant that the golfers played half of their game parallel to the beach and about turned to play the rest home. On many old-established courses the 18th hole is in fact named **home hole**, or, in Scotland, **hame**.

Par

Each of the 18 holes is allocated a par figure dependent now entirely on its length. Not long ago the various clubs could assess by degree of difficulty how many strokes a hole should be completed in, making it extremely difficult to compare how players earned handi-

Below left: A par three hole is one which is less than 240 yards.

Below right: A par four hole is one which is over 240 yards but less than 475 yards.

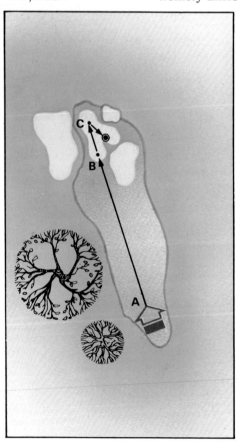

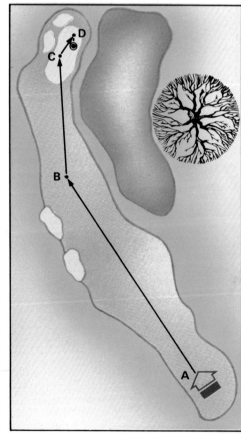

caps. Apart from this, two expressions were used to describe the same thing, namely **par** and **bogey**. Now that yardage is the deciding factor the American meaning of the words has been adopted; par being the number of strokes required by a first-class player at each hole, and bogey when one stroke more, or over par, is taken.

There are three figures, three, four and five, involved in assembling par. Each hole is assessed according to the amount of strokes taken to reach the green, then two putts are allowed.

Any hole of up to 240 yards is a par three. A good golfer should be able to cover up to that yardage in one stroke; add the two putts, making three altogether, and the par is established.

For holes beyond 240 yards, but less than 475 yards, the same player could not reach the green in one – but could in two; add the putts and the par is four.

Over 475 yards it would take three strokes to cover the distance and since golf's long holes are all within the reach of three, the par would be five.

The holes are known as short holes, medium-length holes and long holes.

Below: A par five hole is one which is over 475 yards.

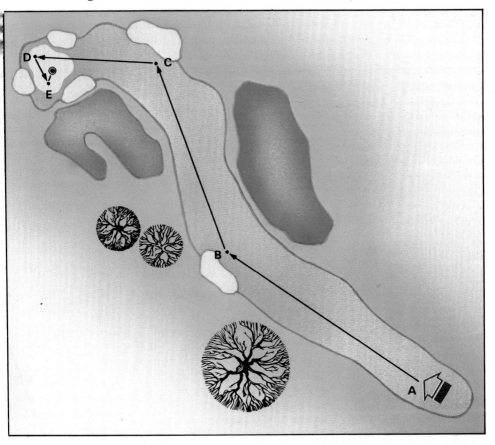

The best courses, where there is no shortage of land, usually consist of four par threes, ten par fours and four par fives; the total working out (at an average of four per hole) at 72 for the course. In ideal circumstances, an equal distribution of par threes to par fives would be found in each of the halves so that a **nine** would be two at three, five at four, two at five. The total for each nine holes is 36.

Handicap

For a definition of handicap, see page 26. Hypothetically, should a golfer play the required strokes to reach every hole and use the allocated number of putts he would complete the course in what is known as a **scratch** round. There are many rounds played where a scratch total is achieved, yet the figures compiled are not exactly those dictated.

A player who drops a stroke, for example at the first hole, has **bogeyed** it. Should he follow that up at the second hole by picking up a stroke on the par he will have **birdied** it and will of course be **level par** once again.

He could, however, drop two strokes to par at the third hole and would therefore incur a **double-bogey**. So, to simplify the mathematics, he needs to play the fourth in two below the par to have an **eagle**, and would once again be level par! There is one more name for a sub par score and that is an **albatross**, which is three strokes below the par. It is *most* uncommon, for it means that a long stroke played from the fairway goes directly into the hole. A hole-in-one stroke which all golfers love to achieve is an albatross, but is often called an **ace**.

So if a golfer should drop a number of strokes to par for the course, the average of those figures will be called his golf handicap, and because of the yardage system of establishing handicap he can play on courses all over the world with players he might otherwise never have played, whether they be expert or novice. Because of this excellent system one can enjoy an even match — which few, if any, other sports can offer.

Each golf club decides on the order of difficulty of holes, and where a handicap difference should be allowed, the most difficult being called **stroke one**, the next most severe **stroke two**, and so on.

A player with a handicap difference of only one stroke playing an opponent would receive a start of one stroke on that hole, marked on the card **stroke index 1**.

There is a slight drawback to the **handicap system** caused by the fact that one course may have all its par four holes in the 400-yard range where another has most just on the 300 yards. The par total will be the same, but the degree of difficulty will be greater on the long course. However, the golf club may have their course assessed for degree of difficulty and so add one, or perhaps two, strokes to the handicaps of its members.

The granting of a handicap to a club member is done by the handicapping committee of the club who have the power to add to or subtract from it by using knowledge gained both in club competitions and in general play. They may, however, only do so until the player is down to a handicap of *three*, for lower than that requires the decision of the county handicapping committee. The cards for such a high standard of handicap must be completed over different courses in competitions where the 'degree of difficulty' is guaranteed.

Rules: bend them but do not break them

It was once said by the late Walter Hagen, a great player from the United States, that the rules of golf were just a matter of applying common sense. It would be marvellous if it were all still as simple as that today. Like every other professional sport golf is fiercely competitive, which makes comforming to the rules even more exacting. A player's version of what is common sense in the middle of a championship, even in a game renowned for the sporting behaviour of its professionals, often proves to be outside the rules and ignorance or misinterpretation is no excuse.

Walter Hagen of the United States. Winner of the US and British Open Championships.

Every professional carries in his golf bag a copy of the rules of golf. In Great Britain, for example, the rules as laid down by the Royal and Ancient Club at St Andrews are printed in booklet form by the Royal Insurance Company, from where all golfers may obtain a free copy. But, however well laid out and clearly defined the rules may be, in many instances in the course of a round a situation arises which seems totally ambiguous and so an illustrated version is also available. Even so, there is a continual flood of correspondence from individuals and from golf club secretaries addressed to the Rules Committee at St Andrews, all seeking clarification.

Unfortunately, in the case of amateur golf at club level, a judgement may have to be waited for to decide the result of an event.

One recent rules problem sent to Scotland was that when player 'A' holed his tee shot at a short hole where he was receiving a handicap stroke from his opponent he was therefore in the hole for *one*, less his stroke, i.e. *nil*, so he must win the hole. However, his opponent, player 'B', played his stroke next and so mis-hit the ball that it skewed off and struck the first player's golf bag which, according to golf rules, meant that he could claim the hole. How could he possibly win a hole which player 'A' had already won by being in the hole for nil? The whole golfing world waited for the decision which for the first time appeared to have baffled the Royal and Ancient. They deemed the hole to be halved. (This rule was amended on 1 January 1980. Now a player whose ball strikes the opponent or his equipment may either play the ball where it lies or replay the stroke.)

The Professional Golfers' Association has a quicker system and when marshals on the course spot a player who is obviously confused they call a rules official who speeds out by buggy. All credit to the professional competitor because whatever the decision, it is accepted without complaint. Sometimes, however, a player is so sure he is in the right that he takes the wrong action in haste. This may lead to a penalty stroke being added or, even worse, disqualification.

Great Britain's Tony Jacklin, playing in an event when at the peak of his form, found his ball in an animal burrow from which he was allowed a free "lift and drop". He did this correctly, within two club-lengths of the hole, but the ball rolled several feet down a bank. He felt that he was gaining too much, having come from a bad situation and rolling into a good one, so he picked the ball up and redropped it so that the ball stopped rolling within the two club-lengths of the original spot. The rule was that it must be dropped within two club-lengths (changed to one club-length since January 1980) and *providing* it does not roll more than two club-lengths *from where* it is dropped it shall be played. This total distance could be virtually four club-lengths from the original spot. Through being too sportsman-like, he paid the price and was penalized.

Bending the rules?
Using the rules of golf to advantage is a player's right. Often it may appear to be bending the rules but the top competitive players do this and it must not be thought of as cheating. Tournament stars, who would never break a rule intentionally take full advantage of rules.

In a Ryder Cup match, Great Britain versus the United States (before the contest structure was changed to Europe against the United States), one American player whose ball had landed in what looked like an impossible situation in the trees claimed that an animal burrow interfered with his stance. To place either foot in that scrape would have meant that he was aiming miles away from the fairway, of that there was no question, but only the player decides where he wishes to hit the ball and a free drop was allowed. The two club-lengths which were allowed then (now it would be just one) were measured off taking the ball clear of the trees but, when dropped correctly, the ball rolled down a bank into water. Another attempt was made to drop with the same result so the player then placed the ball, as the rules state. So from what had been a near-impossible situation he had a clear shot to the green and won the hole. His opponent accepted this action, for in similar circumstances he could and would have done the same.

Rules and etiquette

In golf the rules must be adhered to and, if the high standard of sporting courtesy and good manners which go hand in glove with the sport are to be maintained, so must etiquette. There is a close bond between the two, and the best way to understand their function is to imagine the playing of a game.

Playing is done in two forms: **stroke play**, or **medal play** where the total score is kept and matched against other competitors participating in the event; or in the head-to-head combat, one player against another which is called **match play**. This is discussed in Chapter 7.

To start a game the players make their way to the first hole. An individual, although he may play on the course, must allow other combinations to play with priority. The hole is started on an area called the **teeing ground**. This is a level area, usually slightly raised to aid vision. The **tee** is distinguished by two markers and the player may strike his ball, with the additional aid of a **tee peg** which raises the ball, from an area on or behind a direct line between the markers, in an oblong up to two club-lengths deep.

Below: A player must tee-off between A and B. Whilst he must never go ahead of the line between the two markers, he is permitted to go behind it as shown from B to C, up to a distance of not more than the length of two clubs.

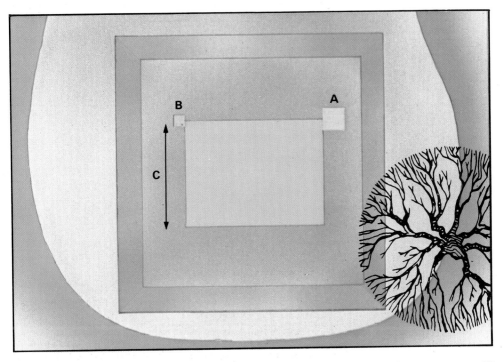

The teeing ground may house three sets of tees: the forwards, painted red, are for the ladies; the middle tees, which are *yellow* and the ones in daily use; and the back tees, normally reserved for tournaments and which should only be used with the club's permission, which are *white*.

Etiquette requires that the player should drive off as promptly as possible, bearing in mind the enjoyment of other golfers. Delay is greatly disliked by good players. Whilst playing a stroke he is entitled to silence from his partners who should, apart from being absolutely quiet and still, be positioned in the correct place. This should be to the right of the tee and behind the line of the ball. Throughout the entire game consideration is given to the person about to play by his partner or opponent who, apart from silent attention, should *never* stray ahead of the ball which is distracting and extremely dangerous. Etiquette is closely aligned to safety, for a golf club may inflict serious injury. When it does, two people are in the wrong. The one who swung it, for he allowed the victim to stand in the wrong place, and the victim for being there!

The first player, decided by a toss of the coin, drives off, followed, in a two-ball match, by his opponent. In a four-ball match his partner would follow him, the opposing team driving off next. Assuming the hole is a par four, then each player would be aiming to land on the prepared part of the course, the fairway, which is normally edged on each side with uncut grass called the **rough**. Often the fairway is bordered by hazards, bunkers, water or, worse still, 'out of bounds', putting accuracy at a premium.

The player farthest from the hole always plays first even if he is on the **putting green** and his opponent is not. The green is the beautifully prepared lawn to which the golfers will be aiming their second shots, and sunk into it is the hole. The greenkeeper of the course changes the hole, which is some $4\frac{1}{2}$ inches across, quite regularly, and daily in the event of a tournament. The top inch of the hole is not protected by the metal cup which is sunk into it to hold the flag upright, so the players should treat the extracting and replacing of the flag with great care, always retrieving the ball with the fingers and never digging it out with the aid of a club! Do remember that the edge of a hole is very easily damaged.

Rough and hazards

Many problems may be encountered during the playing of a hole and many objects, too – some removable, some immovable!

The first trouble spot is the rough and, as on the fairway, the player may rest the clubhead on the grass

Below: Bunkers are known either as 'greenside' (which are found around the putting greens as shown in the diagram, where the player must splash his ball over the face onto the putting green to finish at point B) or as 'fairway bunkers' (which are placed in cunning positions at the edges of the fairways).

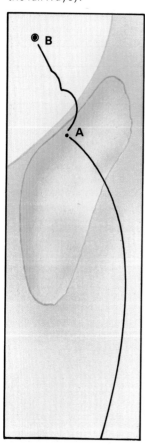

prior to playing the stroke. He may not attempt to improve his position by placing his weight behind the ball, nor may he tap the grass behind it. Only the **tee shot** has this privilege. *In any hazard the grounding of the club or, in the case of water, touching of the water, is never allowed.*

The first of the hazards are bunkers. These are, to use the American expression, **traps** which catch the ball hit off line or mis-hit. Normally, they are rather deep, particularly those close to the green, with soft sand which makes accurate hitting difficult. They also have a steep bank, known as the **face**, in direct line to the green. They are intended to cost the player one stroke, and often a greedy player attempting too much may waste more than one! Whatever the result of his shot, the player must smooth out his footmarks before leaving the sand.

There are two types of water hazard, one of which is called a **lateral**. The lateral is usually a river or a lake which runs alongside the hole, marked by red stakes. The player whose ball goes into this water is allowed to drop it (or take another ball if the original is lost) within two club-lengths of the point where the ball crossed the edge. The penalty is one stroke.

The other water hazard, marked by *yellow* stakes, is normally a lake which lies across the fairway. Removal from this incurs the penalty of one stroke and the ball must be dropped within two club-lengths of the edge, keeping the water between the player and the green.

The player may, of course, choose to play if he can see the ball. Even if the ball is right at the water's edge, the rule of grounding the club must still be obeyed.

A ball in water does not have to be recovered, only seen to go in. A ball lost in other circumstances, or a ball which leaves the boundaries of the course, requires the player to hit another shot from the original spot by dropping a ball there. He counts the one he has hit, adds one penalty and then counts the new one, so in the case of a tee shot he would be playing three. In a tee shot he would be allowed to tee-up the ball. Incidentally, a player may stand outside the boundary and play a ball which is within those bounds.

There is one more kind of water, namely **casual water**. This is a puddle caused by flooding and is not intended as a hazard. The player may lift the ball to the nearest dry spot of relief and drop with no penalty. Unfortunately, if a bunker is flooded and there is no available dry spot, the player can drop clear but must add a stroke.

Other objects

Trees are immovable objects, and any player whose ball is against a tree may deem it unplayable and drop the ball within two club-lengths of where it lay, but *never*

Below: A lateral water hazard, such as a ditch or a stream, running along the side of the hole, is marked with red stakes along its boundary. If a player's ball lands in the water, point A, he is entitled to play it if he can, or, if he wishes, he can drop the ball at point B (two club lengths from the point where the ball crossed the edge of the hazard).

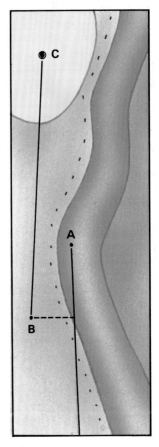

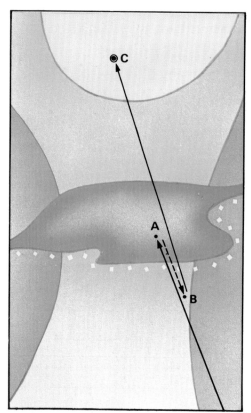

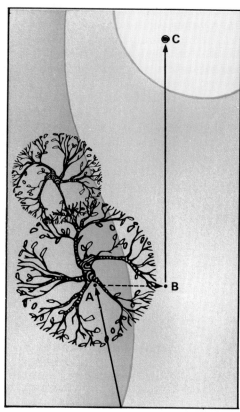

Above left: In situations where a water hazard lies *across* the hole, its boundary is marked with yellow stakes. A player whose ball lands in the water (point A) is allowed to drop back to point B, but incurs a penalty of one stroke.

Above right: Should the ball be unplayable, as shown in the diagram, the player may drop it up to two club lengths from point B, but no nearer to the hole. If this does not help, the player may take the ball behind point A, as far back as he wishes, so long as point A remains between him and point C.

nearer the hole. Alternatively, he could take the ball as far back as he wishes, keeping the tree between him and the hole. Both choices cost a penalty of one stroke.

In a deep forest neither alternative may achieve any sensible escape and he then must take the ball back to the place where he originally struck it, incurring the same penalty as a lost or out-of-bounds would require.

If the object is a tree or a branch of a tree which has fallen, deemed dead, he may remove that but must not dislodge the ball for that incurs a penalty stroke.

There are other objects which are deemed immovable by the rules, such as a rain shelter or bench; in a tournament it could be a TV tower or a grandstand. The player then has the free right to drop the ball but only within the nearest *line of sight.* This may mean taking a ball and dropping it into the rough grass if that is the shortest distance from which the player could see the target. It would then be dropped, but he would never be forced to drop into a hazard.

Dropping the ball

A player who has occasion to drop the ball must do so in a proper way. Standing erect he must face the hole. Then by reaching up and over his shoulder drop the ball so

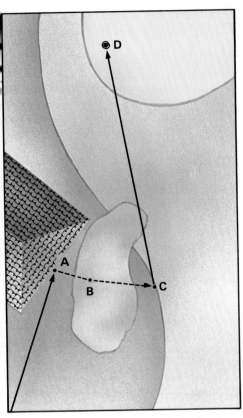

that it makes no contact with his body or his equipment. If it does it must be re-dropped.

Should a dropped ball bounce or roll more than two club-lengths from the first bounce another attempt must be made. If it does so again then it must be placed by the player as close to that dropping spot as possible. A wise player takes care when dropping the ball, for he does not break any rules by trying to drop it in such a way that it has a chance of settling on a good lie.

Once dropped, the ball is in play.

The green

Finally, perhaps after encountering some problems, the players arrive at the green. They do not take their clubs on to the surface but deposit them by the side of the green in a direction convenient to the next tee, thus saving time which could be wasted trotting back and forward.

Before attempting to play any golf on the green, each player locates the mark which his ball may have made on the surface. This is called a **pitch mark**. Professionals would be fined large sums should they be seen failing to repair one.

The correct method is by using a fork which can be

Above left: A player whose ball comes up against an immovable object is allowed to drop the ball one club length clear – without penalty. The player whose ball rests at point A should therefore drop the ball at point B. However, since a player cannot be required to drop the ball into a hazard, he would drop it at point C – beyond the bunker.

Above right: To drop the ball correctly, the player should be facing the hole and standing erect. Should the ball hit the player before it hits the ground, he must drop it again.

purchased from a professional's shop. The turf driven under by the ball's impact is forked to the surface and the whole lot gently tapped down by the head of the putter. The policy in golf is to leave the golf course in the condition you would wish to find it.

A ball may be lifted from the green, not only to repair pitch marks, but for cleaning or at the request of a partner should it impede his path. A marker disc is used and is placed directly behind the ball, *before* the ball is lifted from the grass.

Just as the players are close together on the tee, so they are when they arrive at the green and, since much concentration and study is needed here, silence and stillness whilst one player putts is essential.

The hole completed

On holing-out, the players should replace the flag, which must not be in the hole when the putts are played. Although any player may have it held in the hole as he lines up, the flag must be removed before the ball reaches the hole.

There is no penalty for a putt struck from off the putting surface, but any from the green which struck the flag would incur a two-stroke penalty.

They would then leave the green clear for players following and, in the case of a stroke competition, write up their scorecards, each marking that of his partner. In match play they would decide who won the hole, determining who would drive first at the next tee; the player or team who had the fewest strokes taking the **honour**. In match play the handicap allowance, if any, would be deducted to determine the winner; in stroke play, where the handicap is deducted from the total, the honour would be decided by the best gross score. Should the hole be halved, then the honour would remain as it was at the previous tee.

Outside agencies

Once a ball is moved from where it lies by anyone or anything other than the player, his partner in a four, their equipment, or their caddies, it is deemed to have been moved by an **outside agent**.

At the South Herts Golf Club in North London (which was the home club of the legendary Harry Vardon, the professional who designed the method of holding the golf club used world wide, and which is now the club of Dai Rees, the famous Welsh professional), there was for many years a large crow which lived by the first hole. Regularly, it would sweep down and scoop up balls which had just been struck off the tee. This is the perfect example of an outside agent. Thus, the players were allowed without penalty to place a ball as near as pos-

Above: To attend the flag correctly, stand to the side of the hole, holding the pole at arm's length. Once the player who is putting has struck the ball, the flag should be removed immediately.

sible to the spot from which it was removed.

In Great Britain the main animal culprits are dogs and small boys! In more exotic lands it may be anything from a monkey to an alligator. The agent may simply be a greenkeeper's tractor running over the ball, or even another golfer accidentally kicking the ball in rough grass where he has not noticed it. However, the rule is the same and the player replaces his ball or another if the first is removed or damaged. Incidentally, a ball damaged, whatever the cause, may be replaced at any stage at the request of the player, the new one being placed carefully on the original spot.

Local rules

Most golf courses have special conditions and circumstances which could not possibly be covered by the normal rules of golf; to cater for these, **local rules** are made. These are printed on the notice-board in the clubhouse and are also found on the reverse side of the scorecard.

One final word of advice. Always carry a book of rules.

Below: Here, Neil Coles is putting from the lower level of a two-tiered green. Having his caddy attend the flag makes seeing the hole that much easier.

CHAPTER 2

EQUIPMENT

This chapter is intended to help the beginner choose the right equipment. It will also be of help to more experienced golfers – explaining aspects of different clubs which might affect their shots.

The clubs

Apart from a **putter** which is a law unto itself, the clubs are divided into two groups: the **woods** and the **irons**. The legal maximum number of clubs which may be used during a round of golf is fourteen. There is no minimum number but the performance of a player with only a few clubs would be very restricted.

The normal full set is a choice between (a) three woods, ten irons and a putter, and (b) four woods, nine irons and a putter.

Professional golfers or low-handicap amateurs normally use the set with fewer woods, preferring to carry some of the more difficult but potentially rewarding long irons. The average golfer finds a **fairway wood** simpler and uses the set with more woods and fewer irons.

By a combination of length of shaft and angle of club-face, a different trajectory is created. The club with the longest shaft and the fewest degrees of loft angle is the No. 1 wood, commonly known as the **driver**. The long shaft creates a full arc when the club is swung and the few degrees of loft cause a low trajectory, so the ball flies furthest from this club.

At the other end of the scale there are two iron clubs called the **pitching wedge** and the **sand iron** and with their very short shafts minimizing the arc, combined with the great angle of loft on their clubfaces, the ball spins upwards rather than forwards. Between these extremes, the lengths and the lofts are graduated; a chart of these is shown on page 36 giving the lengths of men's clubs (ladies' being only half an inch shorter per club). Tournament professionals often have a few degrees less loft on each club, preferring to send the ball on a slightly lower flight.

The wood

Woods are so called because the heads are carved from a wooden block which, many years ago, was always of persimmon. Due to shortages and the time it takes to dry out properly, a laminated block was later introduced. Persimmon clubs are still available, and many players who insist that a much sweeter shot can be made from the solid block, prefer them. However, should a flaw exist in persimmon then the whole head may shatter, whereas hidden in one layer of laminate a flaw would remain dormant.

The average weight of a driver is 13¾ ounces; approximately one-quarter of an ounce is added progressively through the set of woods.

The driver is the most exciting club in the game and is used at most of the holes other than the 'shorts'. Because of its few degrees of clubface loft it should only be used when a tee peg raises the ball. Then a player may swing

Opposite: Having the longest shaft and the flattest lie of all the clubs in the set, the driver encourages the fullest of swings.

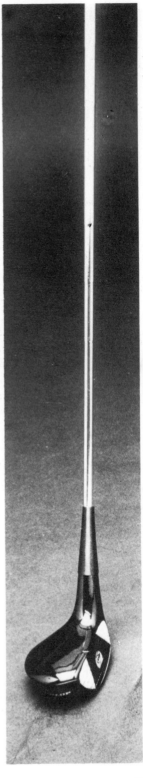

at the ball which can be positioned well forward in his stance (discussed in detail in Chapter 6) causing the ball to be struck on the **upswing** of the club's arc. Without the aid of the tee pegs the driver's loft would be insufficient to raise the ball.

The fairway wood is the name given to the other wooden clubs, Nos. 2, 3, 4 and 5 which, as they reduce in length, become more lofted and heavier in weight. This combination makes them usable from ground level without the assistance of a tee peg.

The iron

The iron club may be hand forged, as indeed they invariably were some years ago, or cast in a mould which gives a much more consistent production and reduces the chances of finding a 'rogue' club.

The head of the iron club is called the **blade** and its leading edge is made to rest at right angles to the direction the ball is to be sent. The shank of the iron, into which the shaft is secured, is angled from the leading edge at varying degrees so that in a set each club in sequence becomes half an inch more upright as its shaft length reduces by half an inch. The longest handle belongs to the No. 1 iron and the shortest to the pitching wedge and sand iron. As they reduce in length they increase in weight, so that a similar swing weight exists throughout the whole set.

Although the pitching wedge and the sand iron are of similar length and angle of uprightness, there are two basic differences. The head of the sand iron is heavier so that it may pass through the sand, and it has a flange on its bottom which prevents it digging in too deeply. This flange is inclined to hit the ground before it should when used from grass and should therefore be avoided on bare ground.

Opposite: Between the long-handled, shallow-lofted blade of a long iron and the short-shafted, extremely lofted sand iron, a great range of shots can be achieved. These are the clubs which bring precision and accuracy to the game.

Below: A conventional set of irons – Nos. 3, 4, 5, 6, 7, 8, 9, pitching wedge and sand iron.

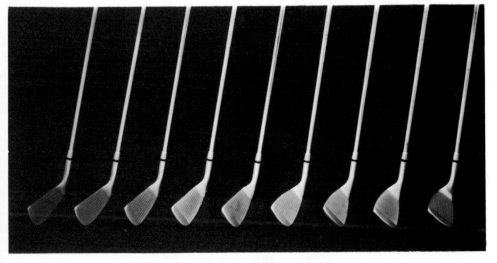

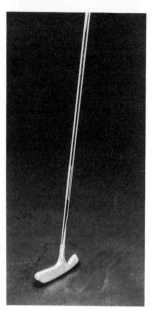

Above and opposite:
Three of the huge range of putter heads available – a consequence of the search to find a piece of equipment which will swing back and forth in perfect balance.

The numbers in a complete set of irons are 1, 2, 3, 4, 5, 6, 7, 8, 9, P.W. and S.I., totalling 11 irons, which would be above the maximum when teamed up with woods and putter. Most golfers do not purchase a No. 1 or No. 2, and start their set off from No. 3. Indeed, special orders often have to be made to a manufacturer to obtain Nos. 1 and 2.

The putter

The putter is such an individual item that it is no longer made with the set of clubs; the choice is varied, with great differences in design. There are blade putters, centre-shafted putters, mallet-headed putters and putters which look like a piece of plumbing gone wrong!

They are all usually of similar length with faces smooth and vertical. The shaft enters the head at an upright angle so the player can get well over the ball. Twists, bends or angles in the design must be made within 5 inches of the sole of the club.

In addition, the balance of the club must be good to roll the ball across the surface of the putting green, and give a good 'feel' in the pendulum movement.

Shafts

There are moves from time to time to introduce new shafts on to the market. Early in this century a transition was made from hickory to steel shafts and much research has gone into perfecting this. Aluminium has been tried, as well as carbon fibre and titanium, and presumably the search will continue. So far the steel shaft has proved the best.

Shafts are graded according to the degree of flex, and the physical needs of the individual player, as follows:

The 'S' shaft is the stiff one which is used by the very fit and strong player.

The 'R' or regular shaft is the one which suits the average golfer.

The 'A' shaft is for the weaker or perhaps older golfer, giving a little more flex than a regular shaft, but not as much as the Ladies' one.

'L' is the reference of the Ladies' making it easier to get more clubhead speed without a lot of physical strength.

Grips

Today's grips are moulded and slipped on over the top of the shaft. Rubber is the favourite grip, although some players still prefer leather, which has to be changed frequently. They differ in size according to the size of the player's hands, and may be varied in thickness by the amount of tape which is used to secure them.

Maintenance of golf clubs

Great care should be taken with golf clubs, for if they

are abused their lifespan is reduced and breakages may occur. Besides, as a financial proposition, a well looked-after set brings about a higher trading-in value when a new set is purchased.

Wooden clubs

These require a fair amount of attention, for should the heads become very wet and be put away in that condition, the wood will swell causing the clubface to go out of true. Headcovers, which should be religiously replaced after every stroke, and not tucked inside the golf bag until the game is over, should be allowed to dry separately from the clubs.

It is important to keep clubs varnished, not merely for appearance's sake but to stop water getting under the **sole plate** where it may rot the wood. The grooves which are cut into all clubfaces to aid spin should be kept clean. If they fill up with dirt or receive an over-zealous application of varnish, the ball may slide off, especially when wet.

Iron clubs

Irons take less looking after; an odd washing of the head, even a little metal polish occasionally, improves their appearance. Professional caddies always carry some sort of implement to ensure that no traces of mud remain in the groves.

Standing clubs in water may trap moisture between the plastic collar and the head causing rust. This is a most vulnerable point which comes in for great stress at impact with ball and turf.

Shafts

These should be wiped dry after playing in rain, and if possible left separated from the wet golf bag since they are chrome-plated and may become pitted and rust. Only very infrequently should metal polish be applied.

Grips

Grips made of rubber may be scrubbed with a nail-brush and hot soapy water which keeps them tacky. Unless this is done, dirt from the fingers impregnates the pores, clogging them and causing a greasy shine to appear. There is no way that good golf can be played using slippery handles.

Leather grips may be cleaned with a touch of methylated spirits, and a little neetsfoot oil rubbed in afterwards makes them last. No matter what attention is given, leather grips never last as well as rubber ones and they are extremely expensive to fit.

Professional servicing

This is a service carried out at all golf clubs by the staff in the professional's shop, both quickly and inexpensively. Home maintenance, however, is often the pride of the golfer and should be encouraged. Repairing clubs is a very different matter and regardless of what is said of

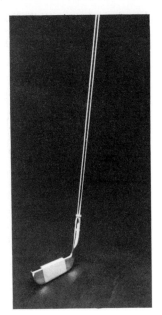

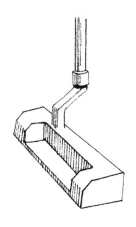

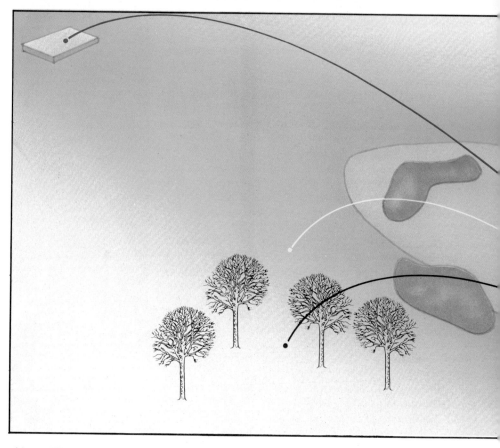

Above: The diagram shows for which types of shot you would use the various clubs in a short set. The wooden club (red) should be used from the tee, and also from the fairway when there is a long distance to be covered. The long iron (blue) should be used when the distance to the green may be covered without using a wooden club. It can also be used for a 'safe' shot towards a distant green, when you are trying to stay short of a bunker.

do-it-yourself repairs, they should be avoided and left to the professional.

Selecting the correct clubs
The beginner

The sensible minimum number of clubs carried would be five: a wooden club, a long iron, a middle iron, a short iron and a putter. These would only be used by a complete beginner, for an experienced player would never attempt golf with so few clubs.

The wooden club chosen should have sufficient loft on it to ensure that as the player improves a little it can be used from the grass as well as from the tee peg – all that should be attempted at first. A No. 3 wood is ideal, having the combination of some degrees of angle on the clubface and a shallow head.

The long iron comes from the group of irons Nos 1, 2, 3 and 4. The beginner should only use either the No. 3 or 4, because these clubs supply the loft required. Thus the 3 and 4 irons can send the ball a healthy distance and should be used, prior to progressing to wooden clubs from grass level, for all long fairway strokes.

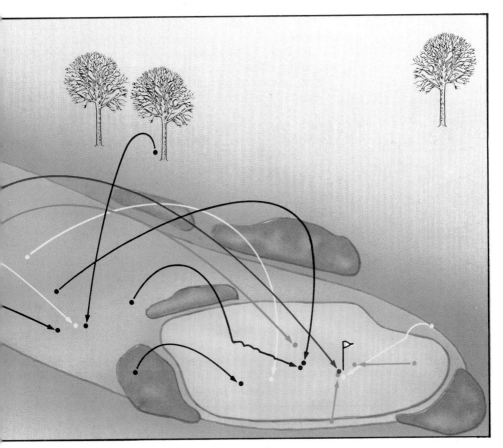

The *middle iron* used would be from the group 5, 6 and 7 irons, any one of which may fill no fewer than three rôles. These are:

1. A club in its own right which the player uses when the appropriate distance from the green.

2. A sensible club to play from a reasonable lie in rough grass so that a fair distance may be covered without risk.

3. When close to the edge of the green, though not close enough to putt, a middle iron is used to play the delicate little chip shot, discussed later.

The *short iron* is chosen from the Nos 8, 9, pitching wedge or sand iron, each of which may have several rôles, as follows:

1. A club in its own right with a normal yardage of flight.

2. A club which is used to recover from bad positions in the rough and hazards such as bunkers.

3. It is used for the delicate pitching strokes, which are lofted on to the green.

The middle iron (yellow) can either be used to play from the fairway to the green, or used to chip from the approaches to the green. The short iron (black) can be used from the approaches to the green or for high approach shots. It can also play many short pitch shots, short recovery shots and bunker shots. The putter (orange) should always be used on the putting green — although, on occasions, when the fringe is very short, it can be used from just off the green.

The putter, which makes up the total of the five minimum clubs, speaks for itself and has only one rôle.

There are disadvantages in having few clubs and doubling them up to perform so many duties. No club can remove a ball from a bunker like the sand iron, and should the beginner choose that as the only short club great problems will arise with the normal grass strokes. However, if there were no disadvantages experts would not trouble to carry the other nine clubs as they do – and they would carry more if only they were allowed!

The argument for a short set is that it teaches the novice to appreciate the different types of strokes and to learn improvization. Many of the young Spanish professionals, such as Severiano Ballesteros, who started as caddies, opened their careers with only a few old clubs and yet are renowned for their ability to fashion strokes. Nevertheless, it is a difficult way to play, and efforts should be made to add more clubs as confidence and ability are gained.

Young golfers

The number of clubs required by a child taking up golf is the same as an adult but the clubs must be lighter and shorter. New clubs, though fairly expensive, are made by all the major manufacturers. Old clubs may be cut down to fit but this should only be done by a club professional who tailors them to the child. When a piece is sawn from the handle to reduce it, it has two effects. It is made lighter, and this is good, but it also causes the shaft to stiffen. It is ideal if the reduced clubs were originally ladies' clubs, for their whippy shafts will firm up without becoming too stiff.

Increasing the number of clubs

The normal progression before purchasing a full set is to buy half a set. Here the player has two woods, one which is exclusively for tee shots and the other for those long strokes from the fairway, and four or five irons; four in the half set with the even numbers giving 4, 6, 8 and a pitching wedge; five in the case of the odds 3, 5, 7, 9 and a sand iron.

The beginner who shows a lot of promise would be best suited by clubs with odd numbers – using a No. 1 wood for a tee shot, taking care that it is reasonably up to date with at least ten degrees of loft (many of the old models have less and are poor). This leaves the No. 3 wood for fairways; the no. 3 iron would also be of use to the more talented beginners.

The less talented would be best off with the even numbers, using a No. 2 wood for the tee shots and a No. 4 wood for the fairways. Instead of having the more difficult No. 3 iron it would be found easier with the extra loft of the No. 4, and so on down the set – bearing in mind that the greater the loft, the simpler the stroke.

The full set

A full set is the final step and great care should be taken in the selection of it. Professional advice is an advantage and any golfer who is not a member of a golf club should feel free to go to the professional attached to one and to be fitted properly, whether the requirement be new or used clubs.

Weight, length and stiffness of shaft are all important and the **lie** of the club must be correct. Thus, it is best if an expert checks this. The lie is the angle at which the neck (in the case of a wood) and the socket (with an iron) comes from the head. Whilst it is always important that a tall person has an upright wood and a small person a flat-lying one, with an iron club it is positively crucial. A wooden club, with its flat bottom, is designed to sweep the ball, but the iron is involved very much in striking into the turf.

A tall man trying to use a flat-lying iron will find that the toe of it strikes the ground before the club meets the ball and that the clubface will twist.

A small man with an upright club must experience the opposite, the heel of his club meets the turf and turns the head in the other direction.

Below: Should a tall golfer attempt to use a club which lies too flat, he will find that the toe of the club strikes the ground before contact is made with the ball. The heel of the club is driven forward and the ball pushes off to the right. A smaller man using a club which is too upright will find that the heel of the club makes contact with the ground before the ball. The toe of the club spins inwards and the ball is pulled to the left.

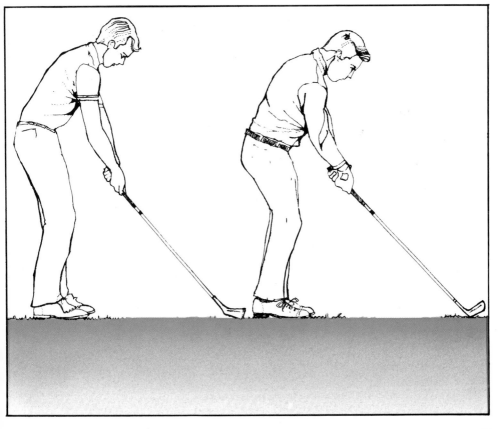

Right: There are several items of equipment which can make golfing much easier. A left-hand glove, for instance, is used by almost all of the top golfers. As the pace of your swing increases, you will also find a pair of well-spiked shoes necessary. A large bag is another useful item, saving wear on the grips of your clubs. A well balanced putter is essential. Once having gained confidence with a fairway wood, you should try using a driver from the tee. Finally, a matched set of irons would be a sound investment.

Other items of equipment

Merchandizing is big business in golf and numerous accessories are produced to meet the demands of golfers, many of which are unnecessary. However, there are many pieces of equipment which are essential and some of them are detailed here.

A small golf bag, which is carried around on the player's shoulder, is ideal for a part set but not for a full set of clubs. Should 14 clubs be jammed together too tightly, the handles will be damaged as the clubs are squeezed in and out. A large bag, which has a hood cover for wet weather, is a sound investment and should it prove too heavy it may be pulled around the course on a trolley.

It is well worth getting a good golf trolley. Somehow in the manufacture of the cheaper trolleys the skimping in production costs always affects the performance.

Good spiked golf shoes are essential, for it is useless to attempt hitting a ball without regard to footing. The athletic movement of a properly executed golf swing requires a stable base.

Wearing a glove, though not imperative, is recommended, for the added support provides the firmness required in the grip when the club strikes the ball. Almost all tournament professionals wear a strong glove.

These are a few of the important pieces of equipment required to play golf and though there is a never-ending flow of new items, many of them are pure gimmickry. One need only acquire what one wishes, and needs.

The golf ball

Two sizes of ball are used and are described as American size which is 1.68 inches, and British size at 1.62 inches. Both, however, have the same weight – 1.62 ounces. In all professional events and the open championships, players are bound to use the larger ball which, although it may appear easier to hit, does show up swing faults more quickly because it is vulnerable to greater spin.

Another innovation in ball design is a choice of two compressions, and novice golfers, or those of average strength, should never use the high compression ball because it is much too hard.

With golf balls it is a case of 'you get what you pay for', but the more reasonably priced are suitable for the needs of average players.

As will be illustrated in the following chapters, there are as many ways of swinging at a ball as there are players. However, the rules of the game (as determined by the Royal and Ancient) are emphatic that the ball 'shall be fairly struck at with the head of the club and must not be pushed, scraped or spooned.'

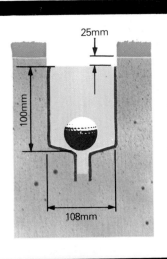

CHAPTER 3

THE
CLUB PRO

The most important role of the club professional is that of teacher. Golf is a sport which simply cannot be played well without good tuition.

In the major golfing countries there are two kinds of golfing professionals. Firstly the **club professional**, dealt with in this chapter, and secondly the **tournament professional**. Both are members of the Professional Golfers' Association (PGA), which in Great Britain has its splendid headquarters at the Belfry National Golf Centre near Sutton Coldfield. As the two perform entirely different rôles they belong to different sections of the Association, although it is possible to be a member of both sections. The members of the Tournament Players' Division (TPD) specialize in earning a living by their ability as players and a great deal can be learned from their techniques by the club professional when teaching the game. This will be shown in Chapter 6 which deals with the tournament professional.

Until only a few years ago it was common for the professional golfer to combine the rôles so that he could be attached to a golf club as a professional and then speed off around the country as a Tournament player. The sponsored competitions and championships were geared to this, being played from Tuesday or even Wednesday to finish on Friday, perhaps with two rounds on that day, giving the competitor time to get back to his club by the start of the weekend. Those days have now gone and both types have become specialists in their own field, the TPD member doing nothing but competing, and the club professional dealing with his club's members.

A golf club has either a committee, made up of members democratically elected by their fellows, or a board of directors, who select a professional. He is provided with a shop where he and the assistant professionals he engages may sell equipment to members and visitors. A workshop is also provided, normally inside the shop, where he carries out services and repairs. He has access to the golf course where he may play, for a fee, with members and guests of the club, and he has priority on the practice ground to give lessons. Although club members have priority in his lessons appointment book, visitors are welcomed. This is important because many people want to find out their potential aptitude before applying for membership of a club.

Because of the long hours which assistant professionals work during their minimum of three years' apprenticeship, it is normally a very dedicated youngster who joins the profession. This dedication is aimed at one day becoming the Open Champion and, although he may not make the grade, all that he learns in the process is put into good use in his teaching career. It would be true to say that the best of club professionals came from the ranks of those who tried to play professionally, but because of the many demands of such a way of life, have

Opposite: There is an orthodox pattern to a golf swing from which variations are derived according to the ability and temperament of the golfer.

failed. His experience equips him well for the work of coaching. Unfortunately, there have been many youngsters who felt that being a good player was not a necessary part of the club professional's duties, and nowadays the PGA have established playing ability tests before an apprenticeship may be completed. These tests precede the final examination into all the other aspects of the job.

Once established as a club professional, he looks after the needs of the amateur golfer. He becomes a teacher, passing on to his club's golfers the benefit of his own tried knowledge of the swing and the expertise he has gained at PGA clinics and in discussion with his fellow professionals. His insight into the game enables him to study the actions of his colleagues in the competitive field, analyzing and absorbing 'how and why'. He is then able to explain to a novice the simple basics which are so necessary to grasp before starting to play. Without that understanding, the beginner will form dreadful habits. He also can quickly diagnose the cause of loss of form which happens periodically to every player. Most of the great players in the world have their favourite club professional to turn to when things go wrong. Faith in

the teacher is essential, and a very happy relationship can be built between him and his pupil.

Golfers are like fishermen except that where the fisherman stretches his hands wide apart to describe the one that got away, the golfer brings his palms to unbelievable closeness to describe the putt which got away!

As mentioned previously the club professional is a specialist at repairing golf clubs, and most of the work is done on his premises, saving time and cost. Apart from the normal repair he can also alter a golf club to suit the player by adjusting its angle of lie or its weight. Unfortunately, many amateurs ignore the advice of the club professional and adapt their swing to suit the club.

Much of the professional's income is derived by selling equipment to golfers, both members and non-members and, when choosing golf clubs, he is the person best equipped to give advice. The game of golf has boomed over the last quarter of a century and instead of containing a few sets of clubs and some bags, the professionals' shops often look more like fashion boutiques where a person could be fitted out with every conceivable item for golf and leisure.

Below: A good club shop will stock everything you need to play the game.

CHAPTER 4

THE PERFECT SWING

The golf swing is built on a 'ritual' sequence of movements found in the same order in the swings of all the world's top golfers.

There is no more dangerous game to teach yourself than golf, for habits formed early in the career of a golfer tend to stick; the damage done by a few months of 'hacking' may well be regretted for a lifetime. It is most unfortunate that the claim of being a natural, or a self-taught player, is often used as a form of boasting, for when one studies the history of any good player who makes such a claim it is generally found to be untrue. He may not have paid for tuition, but without doubt has studied the actions of better players and has enhanced his natural ability by copying. The risk of waiting to find out whether eye and talent is sufficient is too great, and potential golfers should seek the aid of a club professional.

This chapter is devoted to the explanation of the descriptive language of golf as used by the teacher, since misinterpretation often causes complication. It will cover the major stages involved in the construction of the swing and it will be shown how the tournament player demonstrates a good swing. Each stage will be explained and variations discussed.

The experienced golfer may also benefit, for there is no point in searching for advanced techniques or attempting to cure a fault unless a sound knowledge of the basics has been mastered. To search for a fault later in the swing when that fault may exist, as most do, in the **set-up**, would be pure folly. The order in which the club professional teaches the swing is that which must be checked off when a fault occurs, for that is the only way a permanent cure may be made and steady improvement maintained.

Golf is a wonderful game which can be enjoyed by players of all standards, and it is often remarkable how a person claiming to have no talent whatsoever at ball games placing himself in the hands of a good teacher,

Below: The orthodox grip is named after its originator Harry Vardon. The left hand secures the handle against the callus pad of the hand, so that the fingers curl up from below whilst the butt of the hand comes down from above. The right hand is a finger grip, mainly by the centre two fingers, leaving the little finger to overlap the forefinger of the left hand. The variation used by some players is to interlock the fingers rather than overlap them.

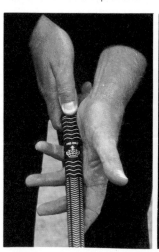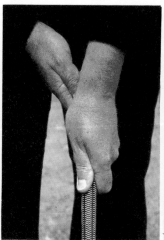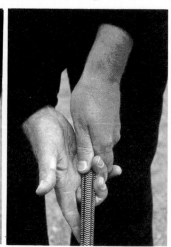

and by sticking to the 'code', becomes a very fine player.

But remember, *naturals are very few and far between and the word should never be used as a substitute for ignorance.*

Part one: the set-up

Setting-up is the expression used by the teacher to describe how a pupil should prepare, prior to commencing the swing. It describes a set of positions that are taken up, promoting the correct movements of the golf swing. Failure to establish these positions is the cause of the majority of golfing faults, so great stress is laid on their establishment.

The order in which they are conveyed to the pupil is exactly that which the tournament professional follows in his preparation, for they are in the form of a procedure which is clearly seen to be applied by all of the top players, in every stroke played. The order, which will be explained in detail in the next few pages, is as follows:

1. The grip is taken up.
2. A relationship is established with the target.
3. The ball is positioned and the stance is taken.
4. The body is postured.

With all these completed, the swing may start.

The grip

Before the hands fit on the handle of the club, the player must establish that the leading edge of the club is at right angles to the shoulders. Then the hands are applied in the form of the **Vardon grip** which has been proved to be the most effective and which, apart from the fact that some players prefer to interlock the small finger of the right hand with the forefinger of the left, has been generally accepted for the past 50 years.

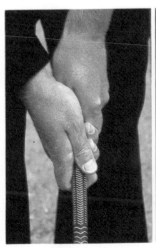  

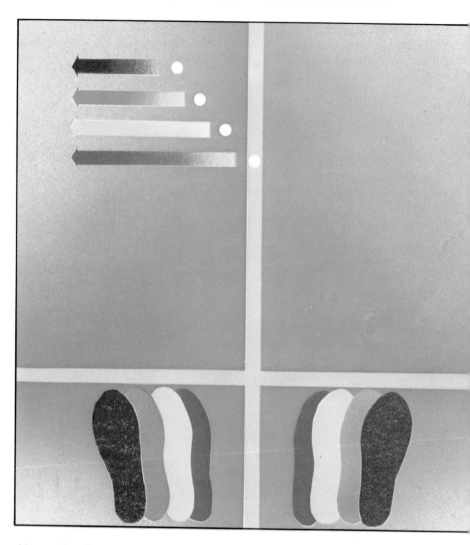

Above: The illustration shows what should be the position of your feet in relation to the position of the ball when using the driver (red), fairway woods and long irons (blue), middle irons (yellow) and short irons (black).

The beauty of this grip is that it utilizes both har The palm of the left hand, which does not have the s of the right, is used to grip the club. This passe strength and authority up the arm and works by **cock** the wrist joint in a simple manner. The right ha however, which is stronger and more flexible, grips club solely with the fingers and the wrist joints ma hinged in a skilful, more creative way. The Vardon g permits both hands to operate individually, but l moniously and effectively.

Aiming

With the grip complete the player must shape up to **target line**, an imaginary line drawn from the ball to flag. The shoulders, hips, and feet will be parallel completion of the set-up. The best method is to sta directly behind the ball, acutely aware of ball and tai

as a line. Then, throughout the process of getting set-up make continual reference to that line.

The ball is positioned and stance is taken

It is important that these two aspects be linked together for positioning the ball, as certain strokes require differing stances.

Playing a tee shot with a wooden club requires a forward ball position and a wide leg stance. The ball is played from a point opposite the inside of the left foot so that it may be struck by the clubhead on the upswing of its through arc. The wide stance makes it possible for the bodyweight of the player to remain behind the ball.

The fairway woods and long irons are played from a point midway between the inside of the left foot and the centre of the feet, in a slightly narrower stance than the drive. This is the base point of the swinging arc and the

Above left: The correct stance and ball position for driving.
Above: The correct stance and ball position for short iron shots.

ball is therefore swept from the lowest point in the arc.

The middle irons are used with the ball only a fraction ahead of centre with the stance just a bit narrower than in wood play. This, though encouraging the player to swing enthusiastically through, still gives a sense of precision.

Finally, with the short irons the ball is absolutely central with the stance fairly narrow; indeed, when pitching clubs are in use the stance narrows to only a few inches. The narrower the gap between the feet, the busier the wrists, essential when backspin is required.

Note: the professionals use a similar stance pattern but most prefer a ball position which remains constant. This is discussed in the chapter on tournament professionals.

Posture

The importance of correct posture is two-fold. Firstly, it must balance the body in readiness for a very athletic movement, where a combination of actions is going to produce clubhead speeds upwards of 100 mph. And secondly, because the angle of the spine determines the angle on which the club circles the body (called the **plane**). If consistency is to be achieved, the angle must be accurate.

With the low point of the swing being in front of the golfer and the high point being behind, the spine must tilt forward. This is the first movement to perfect. The degree of tilt is determined by the height of the player and the club in use. The longest club, the driver, would have the spine at its most erect, with the shortest club, the wedge, dictating more stoop.

The player, therefore, leans forward from the waist, with the tilt of the spine determining the angle at which the shoulders should turn.

The arms hang directly above the player's toes, sometimes giving the impression that balance might be lost falling forward. Only at this point do the legs flex and the hips lower. The balance improves immediately and no harm whatever is done to the spinal angle.

The fact that the right hand must fit on to the handle of the club some 4 inches farther down than the left causes no problem, provided that the player consciously raises the left side of the body and lowers the right. This is not done in an artificial movement, even though many successful professionals lay great stress on it, but by a general feeling that all the muscles on the left of the body rise just that little bit; and those on the right soften down to the same extent.

Posture is the final movement of being set-up, as though gathering the other points under one cover, and if these are done correctly they will fit under very comfortably indeed.

Opposite: Note how Tom Watson retains his spinal angle through the swing.

Part two: the swing

The movements which complete the swing, and which take place from the set-up, all have names and these, in the order they occur, are: the **backswing**; the **downswing**; the **hitting area**; the **throughswing**; and the **finish**. All are formed by the clubhead to shape an arc around the player's body, and all must be executed so that the angle of the arc is capable of delivering an accurate, powerful blow. The angle is a key factor to good swinging and is called the **plane**. The two factors which determine the angle are the height of the player and the length of the club in use. A small man using a long club would require a flat plane, whereas a tall man using a short iron would need quite an upright one.

The tilt of the spine, which is the first movement made when taking up position, determines the angle on which the left shoulder travels below the chin in the backswing, and the right beneath it in the throughswing. Therefore, to find plane, a golfer only has to line-up as though about to hit a ball without a club, point at the ball with the left forefinger, then by turning the shoulders fully, point the other hand in exactly the opposite direction. The angle shown is that on which a correct arc would operate. By swinging a complete reverse movement, so that the hands exchange places, the spine will be seen to retain its angle throughout. No consistent swing can ever be developed without an awareness of plane and a willingness to stay within its protection.

The three headings below relate to initial movements which are sometimes made to aid the start of the swing but are normally used by experienced players. Nevertheless, they should be understood by every golfer for, at some stage or another, tension will come into the swing and it may prove quite difficult to relax and make a good start.

Waggling

The player makes a miniature backswing from the ball, the clubhead moving away about a foot or so, then back to the ball. This is combined with a gentle transfer of body weight from foot to foot. Once there is a feeling of *free* movement, the backswing stroke can be played.

Forward press

This is a favourite amongst the better players. At the last second before the swing starts, the hands, combined with the right knee, push slightly forward towards the target. The recoil sets the swing moving. Gary Player uses this method and claims it gives a greater sense of purpose and determination to his action.

Club clearing

This requires the clubhead to be raised from the turf when lining-up to the ball. A flowing movement is encouraged from this position. Nevertheless, this is a

Opposite: Tom Watson, the leading money winner in golf in 1978, demonstrating a perfect 'set up'.

method for the better player. Hubert Green of the United States specializes in it and is often more than the normal half an inch off: sometimes, in fact, as much as the height of the ball. Howard Clarke, the British Ryder Cup player who found his club sticking, was advised to adopt this method and did so with distinction.

The backswing

The term backswing refers to the movements made to get the club away from the set-up into a position from which it may successfully swing through the ball. It is a pity that the word used is not preparation, which is what the movements are, for backswing has such a final ring to it as though it refers to a complete position, and this has led to many bad actions amongst players who have misinterpreted the meaning. One only has to imagine throwing a stone as a comparison. Throwing the arm back and then attempting to throw it forward to release the stone would produce very little. The hand, wrist and arm should be drawn back quite deliberately, in the correct angle, then launched forward, exactly as a golf swing should be. What has to be accomplished by the time the backswing is completed is as follows:

1. *Hands.* The preparation of **hand action**, which is the term used to describe how the hands, with their quite different rôles, use the wrist joints to get the club shaft to an angle of not less than 90 degrees from the line of the left arm. Less than this would be quite ineffective. Fortunately, the angle is generally greater because of leverage and the swinging weight of the club, but if it is much more than 90 degrees the grip collapses.

Provided the swinger stays within the confines of plane then the left wrist will cock and the right will hinge (as prepared for in the design of the Vardon grip) into a good angle.

2. *The arms and shoulders.* These should only be considered as a team because they perform as one from the very first moment the hands and wrists tell them it is time to move. It is impossible for the left arm to keep either straight, or travel in search of plane, if the left shoulder does not turn to the front. The amount of turn required from the shoulders is 90 degrees, matching the angle of the left wrist as it cocks the club from the arm.

3. *Hips, legs and feet.* The movements made by these, described as the **pivot**, allow the trunk to turn yet remain almost central, as weight is transferred. Whilst their action is important, it should never be exaggerated in the backswing.

The right hip signals the others into action when the first signs of pressure from the trunk being turned are felt. It gathers that pressure to protect the flexed shape of

Opposite: Tom Watson's backswing – perfect technique.

he right leg. A hip swivel of more than half the shoulder turn would undermine the spiral effect of the swing.

The left knee flexes inwards and forwards releasing the heel from the ground as though giving both a rest, courtesy of the right hip and leg, ready for the onslaught about to happen when the bottom of the body comes into its own on the down- and throughswing.

All of these movements outlined above must be careful, yet smooth and fluid. To attempt to assemble them without a sense of balance and rhythm would be little better than to ignore them altogether, and they are completed in an order which accepts these conditions happily.

The downswing

At the point where the back movements have been completed (the top of the backswing) the inexperienced golfer is at his most vulnerable for his body has tensed into a spiral, with the most strained parts being those which have turned and travelled the most. Understandably those parts are naturally inclined to make a violent return to the ball. So the first movements of the downswing are the crucial ones.

A good swing will develop if the golfer uses those parts of the body above the waist to guide the backswing, and those below it to create the downswing, with the first movement a lateral shift of the hips and legs towards the target. Such a movement has the following advantages:

1. It begins the necessary transfer of weight to the left side of the body.
2. It causes the upper part of the body to start its return journey without expending any of the power it has built up.

There is often confusion about the start of the downswing being from the hips and legs, and some feel that this causes the hands to become immobilized. However, provided the player's head remains in a central position, the lateral direction, having completed its purpose becomes a turning movement, leaving the hand action plenty of scope nearer to the ball.

Others suggest that the angle of the downswing journey of the clubhead is changed with the shock of the bottom half taking over from the top. Once again, there is no real danger if the swinger is aware of a good sense of plane, for plane protects the arc and does not permit separation to take place.

The hitting area

This is the base of the arc where the clubhead passes through the ball. It is the point where the club hits the ball, not the point where the player hits the ball. Any conscious hitting will only serve to put the line of the

Opposite: Tom Watson's downswing; whilst there is great hand action in the 'hitting area' of this swing, it is not a separate, conscious movement. The hit is contained within the arc.

shaft of the club beyond the line of the player's left arm, the point where all power is gone. How silly, then, to spend this power prior to reaching the ball.

At the moment of impact the player's intention should be to swing on through the ball. The central position of his head will convey to the prepared wrists and turned shoulders that the hips and legs have done their work and it is now their turn to release power. In a full shot the hand action is involuntary.

It would be totally wrong to claim that there is no need for trained hand-and-wrist action, where the left wrist cocks and uncocks, and the right hinges and unhinges to give a sense of feel and timing. However, the training of this should be confined to part shots and pitch shots and, indeed, should only be used in such shots, or in trick shots. A golf swing contains its hit within its arc, hidden so that an onlooker may not detect it! If a conscious, independent hand action takes place in a full shot the arc will break up.

The throughswing

With the hips and legs now turning towards the target and the club having released through the ball, the player is now ready for the throughswing. This is also a vulnerable point for there is the temptation to feel that, since the ball has gone, anything will do. The ball is not the object in a good swinger's mind, it is the style of the finish and it is to that end that the arc must follow through. The head must be still, and although the face and eyes may turn to follow the ball the position must be retained. It guarantees the valuable plane and maintains the spiral angle right through to the finish.

The arms flow through with the club and should be made to do so, for the fuller the throughswing the farther the ball flies. The impression felt at this moment is that the whole of the right side of the body is flowing under the arched angle of the spine which, with natural enthusiasm, will have tilted slightly more.

The finish

The fullness of the finish is determined by the club in use. It is the **goal** of the swing in a full drive to have the bodyweight solidly up on the forward hip and leg, with the front of the body fully turned to face the target and the club close to touching the player's back. In a short iron stroke, the narrower stance and the limited arc would provide a much more balanced finish with the head looking at the turf marginally longer, thus adding to the sense of precision.

What must be obvious is that the regard for plane exists right to the end and the spinal angle is still felt clearly. Even the eyes look after the ball on the same angle, remaining in the completed arc.

Opposite: Tom Watson's throughswing shows no flick of the wrists, only a determined surge through towards completion. Notice how the spine's angle is maintained through this point.

Summing up: the full swing

Though the swing builds up in pace from the initial starting movements of its backswing to the point of highest speed, through and immediately after the impact, this speed is gathered gradually. Do not make the mistake of sudden, jerky or unnatural movements. A good swing with balance, rhythm and its width of arc protected, will effectively move the ball. Pace is determined by the temperament of the individual: an edgy, highly strung person will find himself using a fast overall movement and will find it difficult to swing deliberately slowly.

The key to good timing in the swing is the pacing of that initial movement from the ball so that each and every muscle involved is simultaneously prepared and co-ordinated.

Below: A player accidentally positioning the ball for each club, too far back in his stance (ie. towards the right foot), would be encouraged to swing the club back too much on the inside. The extra shoulder turn with such a movement encourages a hook.

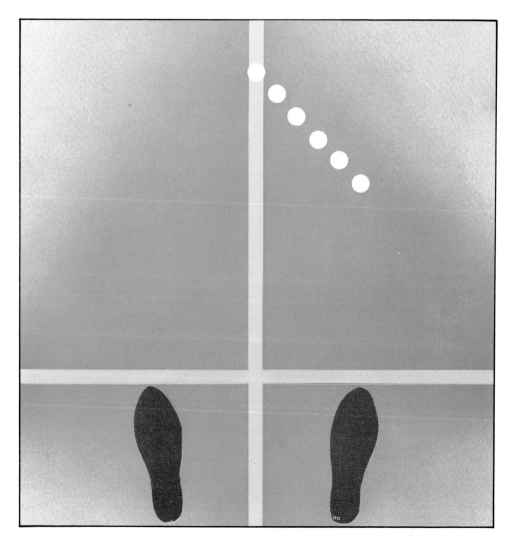

Part three: understanding swing faults

It should be understood that when a good player performs a trick shot which, by its spin, moves the ball away from the original path, he is playing a bad shot intentionally. The next few pages are devoted to explaining what parts of the swing cause variations of flight so that, when required, they may be used and when they happen unintentionally they may be corrected. The journey of the ball is dependent on two things: firstly, the path of the club's arc as it passes through the base of the swing; and secondly, the state of the clubface at that time, which gives the sidespin and determines the curve.

Slice and pull

Slice and pull are grouped by a swing which travels across the target line from *out* to *in*.

What causes a slice? With its two directions of flight the slice comes from a collection of errors stemming from a **slicer's grip**. Here one or both hands are placed to the left of the handle. This sometimes causes the ball to be positioned forward in the stance, which in turn causes the shoulder line to be turned off to the left of the target line.

As the backswing starts the hands have to roll the clubface outwards and open as a means of strengthening their 'weak' position on the handle. They have little chance of replacing the clubface on the return because the shoulder line leads them across the ball on an out to in path.

The ball sets off to the left because of the swing path, then, because of the sidespin from the open clubface, spins away to the right.

What causes a pull? Exactly the same factors as in slicing except that a normal grip keeps the clubface true to the direction of the swing's path, that is from out to in. The ball flies straight to the left.

Hooking and pushing

Hooking and pushing are where the club's arc passes through the ball across the target line, but this time from *in* to *out*.

What causes a hook? A combination of movements causing the ball to move first to the right and eventually to spin off in the opposite direction is called hooking. A **hooker's grip** is the primary cause, where one or both hands are over to the player's right, with the right being described as under the handle. The ball is positioned far back in the stance, encouraging the shoulders, hips and feet to turn off to the right of the target.

As the club leaves the ball in the backswing it travels quickly inwards from the target line, with the grip turning the clubface into a hooded or closed position. Even the mildest of shoulder turns, coming from such an ill-positioned start gains more than 90 degrees from the

Above: The 'weak' grip, common amongst slicers. The left hand shows less than the required two knuckles, and the right hand has taken the opportunity to creep over.

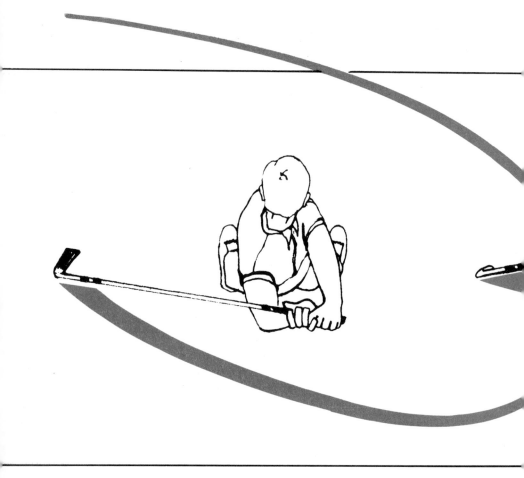

A hooker's grip.

target line, causing the arc to travel back to the ball on an *in* to *out* path. The ball sets off to the right but the closed clubface imparts the spin which brings it back to the left.

What causes a push? Push is caused in the same way as hooking, but a normal grip keeps the clubface true to the swing path, that is from *in* to *out* and the ball flies straight to the right.

Ballooned shots

A player with a hooker's grip in the right hand might get away with strokes played with the ball positioned back in the stance when he crushes down on it, but cannot cope with the more forward position used when driving. As the bodyweight transfers forward the bad grip turns the clubface down even more and the ball is struck with the top of the clubhead, often causing damage to the paintwork on the club as the ball 'rips' backwards. Bad swingers, with this fault, often drive with a No. 3 wood,

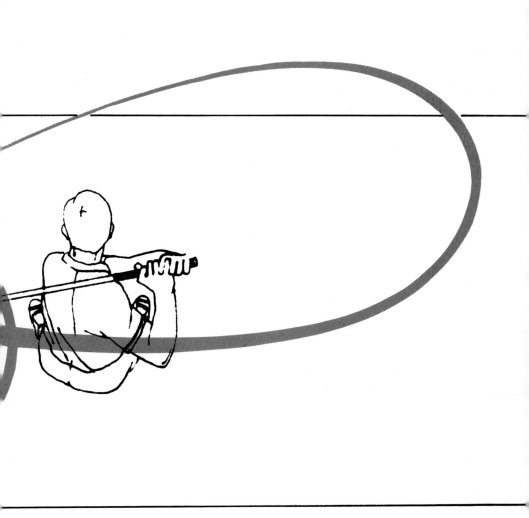

gaining a benefit from the additional loft on the face to replace what they close out, and use a very low tee peg.

Topping the ball

This means that the ball is struck at a point above its centre which makes it impossible for it to lift. This is the most common of beginners' faults.

In the backswing, the pressure of the grip tends to prevent freedom of movement in the wrist joints so the hands do not respond to the wrist action until very late in the movement. By this time the body, and the arc, lift and the inexperienced player cannot always adjust to the correct level.

It is unfortunate that so many golfers believe that topping is the result of lifting the head because whilst this may cause the occasional top, it is not generally the reason, and efforts to 'jam' the head down long after the ball has gone have dreadful results.

Above left: The combination of the hooker's grip and the ball positioned too far back causes the body to 'over-turn' and the clubface to close. The in-to-out arc with the closed clubface causes a hook shot.
Above right: A slicer's grip and a lack of turn of the body in the backswing causes the club to travel across the ball from out-to-in with the clubface open. The result is a sliced shot.

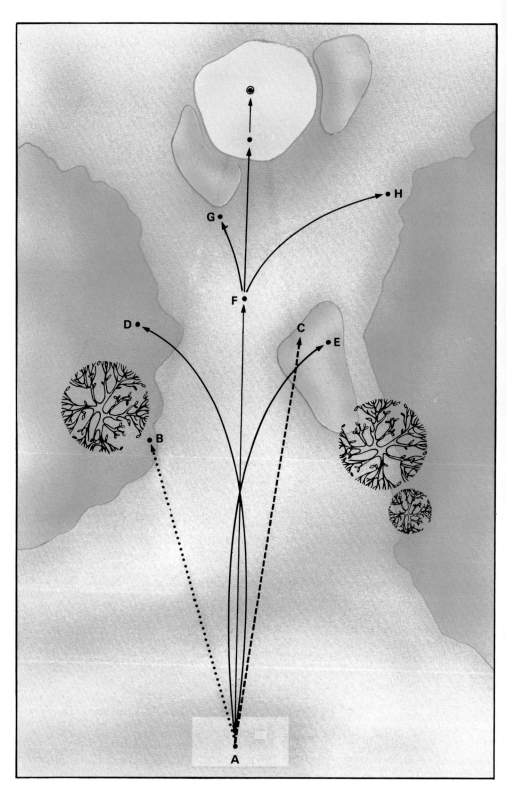

Fluffing

Fluffing is the other fault which plagues the novice and the higher handicap golfer. It is normally caused by looseness. The **fluff** is the club hitting the ground before the ball and is normally seen in the player who introduces too much wrist action too early in the backswing. This causes the arc to leave the safety of good plane and become steep.

Another cause is the belief that instead of the base of the swing being a part of the throughswing, it is a place where an independent hit occurs. Such an attitude produces an early uncock of the wrists, promoting contact of the clubhead and the ball too soon.

Shanking

Sometimes called the curse of golf, shanking is where the ball flies off to the right at an angle of almost 90 degrees after contact with the socket of the club, and seems to be hard to correct. Even the longest-standing of friends do not wish to discuss it because of its infectious qualities!

Once again it is ignorance which promotes fear that makes the shank so dangerous. Because it flies violently off to the right it is thought of as being similar to the slice when in fact it belongs to the hook family and has an *in* to *out* swing path. Attempts to cure the 'disease' with anti-slice actions only serve to make it worse.

The ball is usually found to be too far back in the stance, encouraging an inward movement and a very flat plane. When the player transfers his weight forward, in the throughswing, the arc locks on to the *in* to *out* path and causes the shaft of the club to collide with the ball. It is this which sends the ball off, not a slice spin. Indeed, by attempting some of the movements which promote slice, some improvement would be made since slices come from the toe end of the club.

Opposite: The illustration shows various types of flight – pull (A–B), push (A–C), hook (A–D), slice (A–E), fluff (F–G) and shank (F–H).
Above: Any golf shot can be 'fluffed'. This is when the clubhead hits the turf before the ball.

Part four: hillside lies

Each of the directions in which the ground can slope has a different effect on a golfer's balance and therefore special attention must be given to the lie of the land. Slopes cannot be ignored and allowance must be made for changes in the swing and, thus, the eventual flight of the ball.

Playing uphill

On a gentle slope the player should ignore the natural inclination to lean into the slope with the bodyweight, but instead get as near to a right-angle to it as balance will permit. In this way the club may swing up the slope after the ball and not be driven down into the turf. This adjustment adds loft to the club and the ball flies much higher, necessitating the choice of a longer club than would be normal for the distance to be covered.

The ball should be positioned forward in the stance with the feet a little closer together than on level ground to encourage the player to transfer weight forward up the slope when swinging.

Severe uphills require a greater regard for balance than for distance of flight, and the player will be forced to lean into the forward leg and remain there throughout the action. A very lofted club should be used, as the attack will be very much into the turf and the ball will require a good deal of lift.

Playing downhill

Once again, on a slight decline, the weight is leaned with the slope, for the clubhead should avoid contact with the turf before reaching the ball. This is not easy with the ground behind higher than the ball. It also helps if the ball is positioned slightly back in the stance, which should be taken up wider than normal to discourage the player from walking after the swing down the slope.

Leaning with the slope reduces the degrees of loft on the clubface so the ball flies on a lower trajectory, and the player should select a more lofted club than usual.

One of the most difficult of strokes for any player is that played on a steep decline. He must lean back into the right leg, which makes contacting the ball before the ground almost impossible. However, if a passable shot is settled for, then the ball may be positioned behind, even outside the stance, and a lofted club used to accommodate the descending blow.

The ball above the feet

When the ball is positioned slightly above the feet, on a hillside, a player may be quite adventurous. By leaning slightly back from the slope to achieve a position at a right-angle to the ground, there comes a great feeling of freedom for the swing. The spine is upright and can give more shoulder turn on a very flat plane, contributing to

Opposite: The correct stance for playing uphill (top), and downhill (below).

70

greater power, so the ball may be sent a very long way.

It must be borne in mind that although the clubhead is level with the ground it is not level with the horizontal. Therefore the backspin which lifts the ball will be taking the ball to the left of straight. No player should argue with this but should aim off to the right of the target and allow for the ball to spin left.

Good balance is essential when the ball is markedly above the feet. The player should hold the club down the handle and lean forward to the toes. There is a great danger of striking the ground before the ball if one is too adventurous, so it pays to be careful as far as distance is concerned. As in the gentler slopes the ball must travel to the left.

The ball below the feet

When the ball is slightly below the feet, a player may lean forward as far as balance will permit. The arc will be forced upright due to the difficulty in completing a shoulder turn. All of the elements making up the swing of a sliced shot generally occur when this slope is found, and a slice should be allowed for. Apart from the alterations in the swing movement the clubface is, although level with the ground, out of line with the horizontal

Below: The correct stance to adopt when your feet are below the ball.

and subsequent backspin will take the ball off to the right.

If the ball is severely below the feet, all attempts at a long shot must be avoided – because as the player sits back on the heels to protect his balance, any idea of a swing plane is forgotten and the club is 'picked' up and 'chopped' down through the ball. Only a lofted club with its upright lie has any chance of a good contact with the ball in this situation.

Part five: playing in the wind

Many good players, particularly when engaged in a match against a higher handicap golfer, prefer a windy day, since more skill is then required. The curve on any slightly mis-hit ball will be exaggerated by the wind and soon the striker loses confidence and form. The experienced golfer always uses the wind, as opposed to the novice who tries to fight against it.

Head wind

Into a head wind, the backspin, created by the dimpling on the ball's surface coupled with the loft on the club-face, is exaggerated and the ball soars upwards until, in the case of a very strong head wind, it begins to fly back.

Below: The correct stance to adopt when your feet are above the ball.

Below: Playing into headwind means that the ball will soar and therefore lose distance. The player should use the extra club and attack the back of the green with fairway shots. Downwind, longer distances may be achieved, but allowance must be made for shots to the green to run on. *Bottom:* The easier wind for right-handed golfers is that which blows from right to left. However, there will be a tendancy to get overspin, and shots to the green may well run through. Cross wind from left to right unbalances a player, and causes a weaker hit. Distance will be lost on long shots, though shots to the green may stop quicker.

According to the strength of the wind, the player should select a club which would normally travel beyond the distance required. Then, by reducing the movement in the wrists, shorten the arc. This combination sends the ball on a lower trajectory and makes it much less vulnerable. The ball should be positioned slightly back in the stance (another means of reducing the actual loft on the clubface) but care must be taken or the backswing may start inwards and produce a hooking movement.

Down wind

The down wind is the easiest of winds for it helps fly the ball straight but, although it aids all of the long shots, care must be taken on those approaching the green for all backspin associated with shorter irons will be 'blown out'. Allowance must be made for the ball to run forward on landing. Often, in the case of very strong winds, the ball should be struck to land short of the green by several yards. This may be a problem should there be a bunker in direct line, so the player must aim a little wide, or settle for overshooting the green.

The ball is positioned slightly forward in the stance, which should be narrowed. Extra wrist action is employed in the swing to add to the ball's backspin. The higher it flies the farther it may blow forward and a more lofted club than usual is employed. Besides, it would be

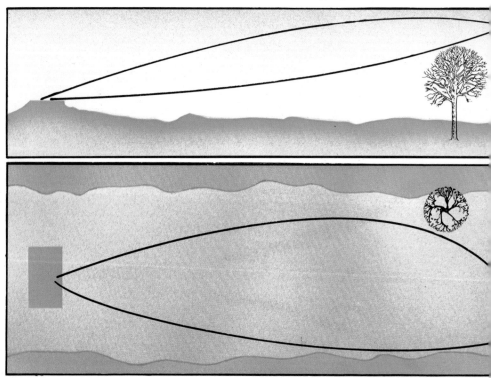

very silly to choose a straight-faced club when a lofted one more than makes up. The initial flight must be *upwards*, or the tail wind will drive the ball down.

Crosswind

Right to left   This is the easiest of the crosswinds for allowing a good hit at the ball because it tends to blow the swinger back towards his heels, making the arc flatter and therefore stronger. Unfortunately this arc is inclined to cause a hook flight which the wind gets behind and the target is missed well to the left. It is essential to aim off to the right to compensate. There can be little hope of backspin and the club chosen should be less than normal for the distance.

Left to right   This is, without doubt, the most difficult of winds, disliked by even the best of golfers, for it blows at his back, tipping the posture too far forward on to the toes and makes a good body turn difficult. The narrowing effect on the arc reduces the power and makes it vulnerable to a slice. In this situation more club should be chosen than would normally be required and the aim should compensate accordingly. Fortunately, the ball has more chance of stopping with its spin coming from a weakened swing, so it may be carried all the way to the green. Nevertheless, it is wrong to be too ambitious in the selection of club – bad balance and long clubs do not go together.

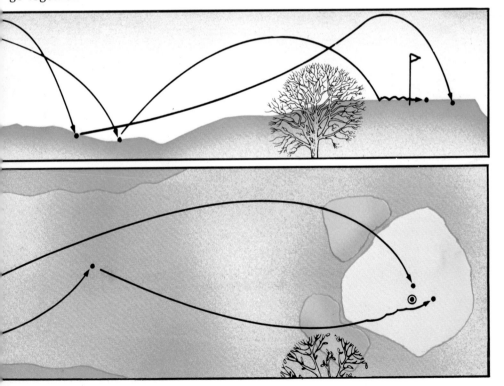

The international set.
Right: Isac Aoki
(Japan).
Below: Severiano
 Ballesteros (Spain).
Opposite: Graham Marsh
(Australia).
Below (left to right): Tom
Watson (USA);
Hale Irwin (USA); Jack
Nicklaus (USA).

CHAPTER 5

THE SHORT GAME

Many players more than make up for deficiency in their long shots with their ability on and around the green.

The ability to pitch the ball high into the air, to skim it low across the ground and to putt consistently well can make even the most mediocre distance hitter of the ball difficult to beat.

One of the wonderful things about golf is that a player of only moderate ability, or of limited strength, may, by skill on and around the green, do more than hold his own against better players. The short game is an area where skill, sense of touch and judgement pay great dividends. When a player is so close to the green that less than a full stroke is required, then the short game begins. It is the art of the part shot; called **pitching** when loft is applied and the ball carries most of its journey in the air to land softly on the green; **chipping** when only a very short distance of flight is required and a greater percentage of run is desired; and **putting** when only a roll across the grass, with no lift whatsoever, is required. **Bunker play**, though a law unto itself, still comes under the heading of the short game.

Pitching

In pitching, all of the muscles which work to hit a full stroke are employed, regardless of the distances to be covered, and any player who feels that by leaving out one part as a means of conserving energy (the footwork for example), will spoil the sense of rhythm. Should such a bad habit be persistently practised the full swing will eventually be damaged.

Pitching should be done with one club, the pitching wedge. In the case of a beginner's part set, the No. 9 iron would be suitable. Occasionally, when within a short distance of the green and more 'stop' is required, a sand iron may be employed, but only from soft grassy lies. The method of reducing the length of the swing, and the subsequent strength, as the player gets closer to the green, depends on three basic factors:

1. Narrowing the stance.
2. Reducing the length of the club.
3. Slowing the pace of the swing.

Sometimes golf seems to be learned backwards, with the full swing being mastered before part shots are introduced, but in order to subtract even percentages of the three given ingredients the player must be aware of what the 100 per cent feels like.

An excellent way of practising is to place about 20 balls in a row then, from playing the first as a full wedge, commence a shot by shot, stage by stage reduction of the three factors. By the time half the balls have been played, the carry will have reduced from almost 100 yards down to 20 yards. At that point the process should be reversed. The impression of coming down a ladder, then going back up again, shows you how co-ordination is maintained throughout the process, and by the time the 20th ball is hit the swing is back in full-stroke condition.

Through this exercise the feet will reduce from being

the approximate width of the shoulders apart on the longest, to only a few inches on the shortest.

At the same time, the hands will travel from being at the top of the handle in the full stroke to about 3 inches from there in the smallest.

Coinciding with these the pace will have been reduced from the strong healthy speed of a full blow to the slow movement of the small lob. This is the most difficult of the three factors, for should the pace drop too low then the arc will 'stall' rather like a motor-car engine when the vehicle travels too slowly for the gear.

Backspin

In a very short time a sense of judgement becomes almost second nature, and the ball can be tossed with great accuracy on to the target. Only then can more positive striking be applied, as done by professionals, and this creates the sharp backspin which stops the ball so quickly.

Above: Pitching the ball well relies on a sense of rhythm – to create the backspin which is a feature of the shot.

Above: Chipping is a more artificial movement than pitching. Keeping the body still – so that the arms, hands and club move 'as one' – is the way to apply the running spin necessary in this shot.

Although much fuss is made by amateurs about back-spin, it should only be attempted when the player is sufficiently far from the green to put a bit of attack into the shot. If only a very short distance is to be covered the player should settle for landing the ball softly from a lofted flight. The danger of searching for backspin is that it requires busy hand action, and at close range other aspects may be neglected and the swing becomes unbalanced.

Chipping

Getting down from just off the green in two strokes is referred to as 'a chip and a putt', and since even the best of players miss many greens with their longer shots, being competent in this department may save many strokes from being dropped.

The most important difference between a chip and a pitch is that in the former the ball need hardly elevate. Indeed, it is its closeness to the ground throughout its journey which makes it simpler to judge. There is little or no backspin on the ball, so whatever weight is given to the stroke is shown in its journey.

Whilst special chipping clubs are manufactured, an ordinary club from a set, say a No. 6 or No. 7, is easily adapted. After placing the hands well down the handle and positioning the ball opposite the right foot of a very narrow stance, the player should lean the club forward to make a direct line from left shoulder to blade. A positive pressure is then applied to keep the wrists in that 'forward-of-the-blade' position throughout the stroke. In fact, it is the artificial movement, back and forth, requiring little rhythm, and no body movement, which gives the shot its consistency.

A No. 7 Iron, used in this manner, will propel the ball forward in a very low trajectory and will carry approximately only one-third of its journey, with the remaining distance covered by running – hence the expression 'chip and run'. It is most important, therefore, to assess the distance which the third would cover and, if the landing point is safe on the green's smooth surface, then a chip is the correct stroke to be played. Should there be any doubt, and the landing spot may be short of the green, then a pitch should be played. However, in certain delicate situations a player who may be happier chipping than pitching can use the chipping method using a lofted club. The backspin given by the lofted blade will increase the share of the total journey which may be carried, and the risk of playing a very low-speed pitch is avoided.

Above: The correct grip and wrist position for a successful chip shot.

Putting

Four dreadful strokes to reach the green at a par five hole can be cleaned from the sheet by holing one good putt, and there are many golfers who destroy their opponents with great regularity by doing just that. Having a putting touch is a great asset; although many insist there is no way this can be learned, that is not completely true. There are certain accepted facts to which all the best-known putters adhere, and once those are learned a player may adapt personal variations.

The grip is adjusted to allow both thumbs to rest on the top of the handle; a reverse overlap, where the forefinger of the left hand covers the little finger of the right, is best. The effect of this positioning is that both wrist joints may hinge where the conventional left-hand grip, turned to show two knuckle joints, causes that wrist to flex.

Because the shaft of the putter is the shortest of all, and emerges almost vertically from the head, the player must get the shoulders well over the ball, which is positioned well forward – opposite the left foot, in a stance which is fairly narrow.

Above and opposite:
Smoothness is the
essence of a good
putting stroke,
something encouraged
by the reverse
overlap grip.

Although feet and hips may be aimed 'off' line to the left, it is essential that the shoulders are in a line parallel to the intended journey of the ball. This is easily calculated, for with such a forward-leaning posture the player's eyes are almost looking directly down on the ball and the path to the hole is easily seen.

In striking the ball there is as little body movement as possible and, although the wrist joints are positioned to hinge, it is only in long putts that they would be consciously engaged. Consistency comes from a low stroke, where the putter head travels back, then through with no jerky point of acceleration – the backswing and throughswing being the same length. Both are completed as close to the grass as possible. Such a movement can only come from the arms.

There are probably more gimmicks produced as aids for putting than for any other aspect of the game, largely because putting may be practised at home, in the office or, indeed, anywhere there is a smooth-carpeted surface.

Learning to 'stroke' is important and keeping its back and forth movement as though on rails is the key factor. However, a pair of straight edges, such as a couple of books set apart, with a parallel corridor just a little wider than a putter's head aiming directly towards a target, will do the job. With the ball placed at the end of the corridor nearest the target the player should guide the back movement of the stroke safely down the passage, without touching either book, then smoothly stroke through in the opposite direction. Accuracy gained over very short putts will continue into longer ones as the natural hinge of the wrists adds to the basic arm movement.

Bunker play

Although many bunkers are situated well away from the greensides, and are called fairway bunkers (or traps), most of the skilled bunker strokes are played from those around the green. Indeed, even when a long way from the green, a player almost always has to accept his punishment and play a short greenside type of stroke safely from the sand. Only on the odd occasion does a ball sit up in sand sufficiently far away from the high face of the bunker for a long shot to be hit. When it does then a conventional golf stroke is played, with common sense suggesting that the choice of club should have sufficient loft to be sure of clearing the lip. So it is that bunker play comes under the heading of 'the short game'.

Ordinary sand

It is essential that the golfer gets the ball to climb sharply and the following steps must be taken:

1.   The leading edge of the blade is turned slightly open with a normal grip taken up, as though unaware of the out-of-line clubface.
2.   The ball is positioned well forward in the stance, which is fairly narrow and is aiming off to the left.
3.   The posture should be very relaxed and, unlike other golf shots, the shoulders are allowed to stray to the left, parallel to the toes.

The arc is made full, loose, and unhurried. Any sudden acceleration will cause the clubface to close, knocking the ball forwards into the face of the bunker. Instead the hips and legs should softly lead the clubhead through the ball. Contact with the sand is made about an inch before the ball and all the movements continue to a full follow-through.

Novice golfers always fear that a follow-through will send the ball too far, but they should understand that it is possible to follow through without speed, and it is speed which makes yardage.

Opposite: A ball buried in heavy sand requires a much more 'heavy-handed' attitude. Your stance must be moved forward so that a descending blow can be delivered deep into the sand. Backspin cannot be achieved in this shot, so allowance for run must be made.

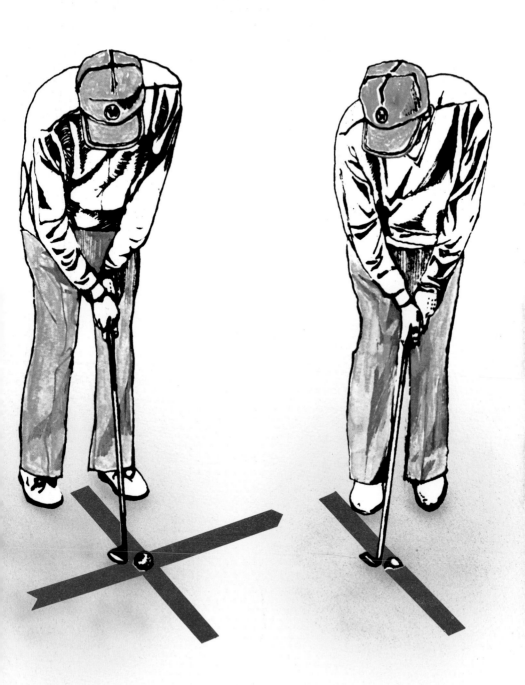

Very soft sand

When the ball is embedded deep into soft sand the tactics used are the same as in ordinary sand, except that contact must be made with the sand as much as several inches before the ball. The bottom edge of the blade must get below the lowest point of the ball and this could be quite deep down. Intelligent aggression must take the place of rhythm, and effort must be made to keep the blade open even when the journey deep into the soft sand forces it to close. In the case of a very foul lie, where the ball is virtually buried, it is often necessary to shoot to excavate as much sand as possible out of the bunker, in the hope that the ball will go with it. Then the stance, aim and blade would all be squared up.

Wet sand

Should a sand iron be laid open, its flange is bound to make first contact with the sand which, if wet or soggy, would cause it to bounce, catching the ball too high up. The player should position the ball more centrally in the

Below and opposite:
It is essential not to panic when close to the face of a bunker, no matter how steep. Open your stance more, open the blade more and always attempt to swing 'across and through the ball'.

stance and bring the whole line parallel to the target line (square). A narrow stance will cause the necessary steepening of the arc, and a little bit of early wrist-break in the backswing will also help. However, this is the most difficult bunker shot since the strike into the sand has to come so very close to the ball.

Often the ball plugs into wet sand and the player has to get the blade down into it just before the ball. In this case there will be no backspin in the ball's flight and **run-out** must be allowed for.

Putting, chipping or pitching from a bunker

Sometimes, when the face of the bunker is very shallow, it is tempting to attempt to hit the ball cleanly, giving it the weight which would be used from the grass. Many golfers try putting it out or chipping with a club that has little loft. Others try a straightforward pitch shot. To attempt any of these is extremely risky and they have a very low success rate. It is far better to perfect a conventional 'splash' type of stroke, and use it.

Above: There are occasions in bunkers when finesse has to go. To get out is more important than the amount of sand removed.

Opposite: Tommy Horton blasts from a bunker at Woburn whilst defending his Dunlop Masters title.

Overleaf: Ben Crenshaw, USA (top left) ; Hale Irwin, USA (below left) ; Geoff Goodwin, Great Britain (top right).

91

Above: Graham Marsh
(Australia).
Top left: Bob Charles
(New Zealand).

Below: Peter Oosterhuis
(Great Britain).
Below left: Isac Aoki
(Japan).

CHAPTER 6

THE TOURNAMENT PRO

Tournament professionals
are more than entertainers;
the benefit of their
techniques and skills is
passed on to the amateur
golfer via the teaching
professionals.

The tournament playing professional earns his living entirely from his ability as a player, and from fees arising from the contracts his talents win him. He is a member of the Tournament Players' Division (TPD) of the Professional Golfers' Association (PGA). He could be an established club professional or an apprentice who applies to the TPD and thus competes to gain a player's card. This is awarded after a satisfactory examination of his playing ability over different courses, and only a limited number of places are available. The successful applicant may join the ranks and compete during the ensuing year at the end of which, should he not have progressed up the list of competitors, the card is withdrawn and must be regained in the same way the following year.

The other method of joining the TPD is from the ranks of amateur golf. Players of a handicap of one or less may apply to the TPD for the playing test and the same conditions then apply to them as for converting professionals. The competition is extremely fierce, and many a reasonably talented youngster who would make a fine club golfer tries and fails, falling into a no-man's land. He cannot compete professionally because he has no card, and he is no longer an amateur for there is always prize money in the qualifying event which means that he loses his amateur status the moment he applies for entry.

Thus a youngster must be sure that he is very much above average. It is for his own protection that he considers the consequences of mediocrity which, even if he scraped through, would prove a financial nightmare!

In Britain a TPD card-holder may not take up a position as club professional until he has completed at least four years with a card and is also capable of passing all the stiff examinations set by the Club Professionals' Division of the PGA. This is only common sense, for the dedication and single-mindedness required to make a successful tournament player separates him from more objective knowledge of swings and techniques – qualities necessary in the club teaching professional. He is far removed from the basic problems of beginner golfers and the bedside manner required in dealing with them. Indeed, it is from his determination and mental control, together with his skill under exacting pressure, which armchair enthusiasts watch at home, or at tournaments, that so much is learned.

The lady tournament professionals acquire their position more or less in the same manner, although the two sexes, as a rule, never compete against each other. In the United States they come under the heading of Ladies' Professional Golfers' Association (LPGA), and for some reason the equivalent in Great Britain, formed in 1978, is the Women's Professional Golfers' Association (WPGA).

Opposite: Nancy Lopez, who is rapidly establishing herself as the greatest ever lady golfer, demonstrating a perfect swing. Using the Vardon grip (interlocking version), she first establishes a relationship with the target. The ball is positioned and the proper stance adopted. She strikes through the ball, full and wide, and continues with the perfect follow through – the spine's angle the same as when the initial 'posture' was taken up.

Opposite and above: The joy of winning the 1979 Dunlop Masters at Woburn shows on the face of Graham Marsh of Australia, after holing out for a final hole birdie to beat Neil Coles of England and Aoki of Japan.

The successful tournament-playing professional is one who masters both parts of golf. The first is the mental approach, for without concentration and self-control he could not score consistently, nor withstand the pressures of each tournament. These last for at least four rounds, one per day and each of about four hours duration. The other is a physical command of the golf swing – to be able to repeat basic strokes with regular accuracy and to have sufficient flair to recover when necessary. He must have the physical strength to hit the ball long distances, yet have the finesse for the delicate small strokes.

Part one: the mental approach
Positive thinking
There is much to be learned from the mental approach of a leading professional. The prime factor is that he is

always positive, and even when things look black for him he wastes no time wondering about what might have been. He is concerned only about the most sensible thing to do. He is prepared to take risks, to drop one stroke if necessary rather than panic and waste even more.

The attitude to his own particular swing is equally positive, and if it works for him then he uses it regardless of criticism. So many golfers fear their swing does not conform with the accepted orthodoxy and end up with a method which, hampered by self-consciousness and caution, achieves little or nothing.

Learning to score

Scoring around a golf course is a habit and players, be they professional or an average club golfer, tend to score a total within a stroke or two every round. One day the total may shoot either up or down, but normally there is a consistent average. The professional believes in averages for they are borne out round after round, and this gives confidence when a couple of strokes are dropped to par, for just around the corner an eagle may happen. One only has to read tournament results to see how often a disastrous outward nine is followed by a brilliant inward, or how a dreadful opening round is followed by a record-shattering second.

A club golfer will recall over his first years at the game how he scored at a consistent level and acquired his handicap. Then, one day, to the dismay of his opponent, he played to a figure far below anything he had ever achieved previously. From that day, although he may not repeat that shock performance he finds a new level, rather like a plateau, and he stays on this for some time until the same thing happens again. These stages come just as the end average result comes to the tournament professional, when he accepts the average principle.

Wasting strokes

The tournament player does not think of a stroke which gets him into trouble and produces a situation which needs retrieving as a wasted stroke. Not, that is, if it went where it did as the result of a mis-hit or a piece of misjudgement. These will always happen, for golf is very difficult and every player has a share of bad strokes. To him a wasted stroke is one which was played without proper thought. A stroke played in anger or panic, or perhaps out of frustration from missing a small putt is a wasted stroke.

Trying to play a shot which has no chance of achieving an advantage is a wasted stroke: for example, making an attempt to carry the ball over an obstacle when the green is not within reach anyway. Positive thinking would have had the stroke played short or wide of the obstacle leaving a much simpler next stroke. Two shots were needed anyway, so why end up in pointless trouble?

To hack a ball out of shrubbery would only be attempted if there was any way of getting a major advantage. A lift out of two club-lengths for one penalty stroke is the same as getting it out a few more yards with a hack and, if the hack is unsuccessful, then that is a wasted shot.

Attacking the hole with a putt when the green is fast and the putt is downhill would be stupid. There are many occasions when the tournament player will roll the ball towards the hole and settle for two putts. This may sound a negative approach but indeed it is not, for the third putt would, in this case, be the wasted one and that is how many could be taken from thoughtless action.

History will always recall the young Japanese professional Nakajima who took nine strokes to complete the 17th hole (Roadhole) at St Andrews in the 1978 British Open Championship, when within one stroke of the lead. His second stroke to this difficult par four hole reached the green and was within a few feet of the flag when it toppled back into the deep road bunker. The correct thing to do was to play quite positively away from the flag into the fullest part of the green from where two putts would have given him a five; who knows, he may have holed the first. Unfortunately for him he attempted, with his third shot, to get the ball so delicately over the edge (knowing how slippery the green's surface was) that it fell back in beside him. His fourth, fifth, and sixth shots all did exactly the same, until finally he played to the wider area and scored a nine. Surely the perfect example of wasted strokes!

Below and overleaf: Usually a tournament professional will search for the safest route to escape from a difficult position, but not always. Here, Bob Charles, one of golf's most reliable players, makes an attempt to recover too much and pays the price.

To the tee shot

There used to be a saying, 'You drive for show and putt for dough', which implied that it was perfectly all right to blast away with a driver provided the concentration was saved for the putting green. At that time a player was considered to be a bit cowardly, when playing a narrow hole, if he used a much safer iron stroke from the tee. That attitude has gone from the game and the modern competitor thinks about positioning his tee shot rather than just hitting it as hard and as far as he can.

What the tournament player looks for when he steps up on to the tee is the pin position on the green, not just at the short holes but at the middle-length holes where his second stroke must be hit at the green. A long hitter who is capable of reaching long holes in two also looks ahead at these. He is looking for the best line of attack to the flag for the second stroke. Should the flag be tucked behind a huge bunker at the right of the green it would be best approached from the left of the fairway. If, perhaps, a huge tree overhangs the left of the green the player would then much prefer not to have his ball flying into the branches and would come in from the right of the fairway.

Having assessed the best line, he would have to examine the landing area where his tee shot would come down. Many good golf course architects have positioned some sort of a hazard to catch the player looking for the easy approach to the green. This could, for example, be a large bunker at driving length (which would be about 250 yards out from the tee). The player has to make the decision: to play safely past the hazard and face the problem of that greenside bunker or tree with the next stroke; or to play short of the hazard, preferring the open but longer second shot.

Keeping the ball in play is the key to good scoring and the consistent money winners play for position every time.

The tee shot

The professional always tees his ball on the side of the teeing ground so that he can drive the ball away from the troublesome side, even if it makes only a few feet of difference. In the case of an out-of-bounds fence running down the right-hand side of the fairway, it is comforting to tee the ball on the right of the teeing ground and hit away from the obstacle.

Going out-of-bounds from a tee shot worries the professional more than any other mistake. The penalty is high, incurring an additional two strokes on the score, as well as having to play the stroke again with the additional fear of doing the same thing all over again. In this situation a long iron is often chosen because even though it carries a shorter distance, it is much easier to send straight.

Many players prefer to put a spin on the ball as their positive contribution to steering clear of trouble spots. With trouble on the left of the fairway then the tee peg is pushed very low into the turf. It is almost impossible to hook a ball to the left with the small degree of loft on a driver when the ball is tight to the ground. A slice to the right is almost inevitable, and the professional does not

Below: Bob Charles tees off from the elevated second tee at Woburn. This shot was played to land short of the hole, Charles preferring the uphill putt for two rather than the downhiller on this sloping green.

mind a slightly inferior stroke which travels safely into an advantageous position.

Just as it is difficult to do anything but slice with a driver from a low tee peg, it is equally difficult not to hook with a lofted wood (a No. 3 or 4) from one. So, when the out-of-bounds lurks on the right, the professional rejects the thought of a long, long drive and hits with the more lofted club, happy to sacrifice a bit of distance to be positively on the safe spin for the left of the fairway. Remember: *stay in play and make it pay.*

To the fairway shot

Only occasionally from the fairway, perhaps when high trees are in the way, would a professional play deliberately short of a green which was within his reach. Otherwise he would attack the green. However, he might not automatically attack the flag. There is a different attitude to a pin position which is safely in the centre of the green to one which is placed dangerously close to trouble.

When a golf course is set out for a major event many of the flag positions, particularly on the final day of the event, are cunningly, almost cruelly placed, tucked behind bunkers or just on the brink of a huge slope. The experienced campaigner divides the green into three sections, the front, the centre, and the back, and, knowing which section the pin is placed in, plays for the

Below: Bob Shearer of Australia using a driver.

safest part of that section. Greens are normally long rather than wide, and to be in the centre of the correct section means being within a few yards of the pin.

'Playing to the percentage of the green' is the expression used when attacking the pin would be folly. The Masters Tournament at Augusta, in the United States, is one of the great character tests because many of the greens are almost entirely surrounded by water hazards. The pins are in the front section of the greens where the lake is in front of the green, and at the back when the water is also at the back. The players are tested to the limit and occasionally one throws away the percentage rule by attacking those pins. It comes off one day and he makes a fantastic score; the next day it does not, and he disappears.

The tournament professional knows exactly how many yards he is from the green for he or his caddy will have paced the course in advance. He also knows how many yards the pin is from the front and side of the green, for he is given a daily chart showing this information. From hours of practice he knows exactly the distance he hits a good shot with each club in his bag. Thus it is a case of accurate computation, adding or subtracting for wind velocity, selecting which section of the green to pitch on, and then swinging the correct club.

On many of the small British greens the pin is never more than a few yards from the centre of the green.

Around the greens

The professional is interested in one thing when he is close to the green and that is 'how many'? All that matters is getting the ball on to the green so that if it does not go into the hole it stops so close that the remaining putt will be a formality.

Like all players, regardless of handicap, the professional will use his putter if he can – even when not on the surface – provided the grass is very short and the ground dry and firm. For the putter is reliable *and a bad putt often rolls closer than a good pitch.* In the closing stages of the 1977 British Open Championship at Turnberry, Tom Watson, the winner, holed a putt for a two from the edge of the rough, having to roll it across a dry bank before it even reached the green. This confounded Jack Nicklaus, who was waiting on the green only a few feet from the hole with his tee shot, and it virtually decided the result there and then.

The major difference between the professional and the club golfer is in the choice of club he would use when almost within putting distance. Should there be no real trouble between ball and pin the professional would run the ball close to the ground as usual, but, the moment there appears a little bank, a slight gradient, even a little moisture, he selects his own particular

Opposite: Three of golf's best exponents of their favourite shots – Neil Coles pitching, Graham Marsh putting and Isac Aoki chipping.

favourite club. This may be any club from a No. 9 iron, pitching wedge or sand iron, but it will be one with which he has hit thousands of practice strokes. Gary Player carries as many as three different clubs for pitching, all of them against just that particular eventuality. Neil Coles has a favourite old sand iron with which, defying all logic, he pitches off the barest ground. Manuel Pinero, the brilliant Spaniard, has had to stop practising with his favourite wedge for he was in danger of wearing out its face. The confidence gained from continually working with one club allows all types of strokes to be played with it. Even with the loft of the sand iron, by the skilful adjustment of wrist action a ball may be made to fly very low and have the advantage of the backspin from the loft.

The attitude of, among other current players, Nick Faldo, who is another who 'sand irons' in from any position, is that when the ball is in the air you know what it will do; on wet grass, or going up slopes, you can never be sure.

The ability to line-up to the ball with the hands forward of the ball and then go through the ball that way, demands a disciplined sense of purpose. The slightest hesitancy would have the clubhead flicking through too soon, and it would collide with the turf before the ball. And even if it got to the ball it could not create backspin from such action.

The lesson to be learned is that, although the code which this book presents in Chapter 5 (The Short Game) should be adhered to, you should be adaptable and have confidence in your choice of an unorthodox club. Find your favourite, and work with it. If things get sticky, it may give you extra confidence.

To the putting green

There are many sayings describing the art of putting. One is 'miss it on the professional's side'. It is a sensible expression which probably would have been put more positively had it been 'hole it from the professional's side'.

When a professional studies the line on the green by crouching down behind the ball and looking towards the hole, he is searching for the slope of the green. Should this be very subtle it may be missed even by the experienced eye. Some competitors use the plumb-line method of holding their putter lightly at the tip of the handle to allow the shaft to fall vertically so that the slope of the green shows up against it. Once the slope has been detected, the player works out how much he must set his ball off-line in its initial direction to allow for the downhill curve it will eventually make. He hopes to 'borrow' the correct amount; professionals know that over-borrowing leaves the ball likely to take a last-

Opposite (top): For once, the pitching wizardry of Neil Coles lets him down and leaves him with more work to do on the green than he would wish. However, the putt is rapped firmly home. *Opposite (below):* Vicente Fernadez of the Argentine who won the PGA Championship at St Andrews, his skill on the putting green more than making up for his slight frame in the gale force conditions.

Overleaf: Gary Player. Although in his forties, he is still regarded as one of the toughest competitors in the game. He has the ability to shrug off foul conditions as if they did not exist. The umbrella in the picture is to cover his equipment.

second topple into the hole, whereas under-borrowing has no chance.

There is a little more to reading the amount to borrow and this is why time, care and trouble should be taken in lining-up a putt. If there is a slope on, say, a 10-foot putt, requiring a borrow of 4 inches, a professional would pick a spot exactly that distance to the top side of the hole and roll his ball towards it. Should the putt be downhill, he would double the amount he borrowed, for the gentler the roll the more the toppling weight of the ball exaggerates the turn. In reverse, on an incline he would only aim 2 inches topside, for his firmer rap at the ball would drive it on a more direct path.

One very important point to be learned from the professional is how carefully he watches the last few rolls of his putt, for in those final turns the slope of the green has its greatest effect on the course of the ball and if he does not hole the first one he gets a very clear idea of just how the ball is going to turn on the next putt. *Look and learn!*

Combatting the elements

The tournament professional is committed to playing whether the weather conditions be fair or foul. Only circumstances such as an electric storm, fog or flooded greens where holing-out becomes impossible, stop a competitor from playing. The decision is made by the tournament committee and the competitor marks the spot where his ball rested, to continue when the weather improves.

In diabolical conditions, the player who does well is the one with the determination and temperament to accept them and get on with the job. Golf is very much an attitude of mind in these circumstances, just as in any other sport. In soccer when the pitch is frozen, the team whose manager rushes about complaining that the ground is not fit gets his players so convinced they should not play that when they do they are likely to lose. Any golfer who keeps waiting for the siren to sound, who believes that there is no justice for it to rain on him when the players who were drawn out in the morning enjoyed sunshine, who believes that no-one can play with wet handles, will do so to his cost. There is usually someone who can do all the things he believes cannot be done, and who makes the best of it and gets round. A top professional knows that if he had to play a round up the main street, using a couple of spades and a sweeping brush, someone would do it well! So why not him? This attitude is a necessary part of playing golf.

Accepting the conditions and adapting to them is essential: arguing with wind and rain just does not work. Should the club used have insufficient loft the ball has difficulty climbing up through a deluge and it is also inclined to slip on the clubface, so the professional

sacrifices a bit of distance and chooses a club with more loft on the face. A No. 3 wood from the tee is much more successful than a driver and, should his hands slip a little bit in the wet, the clubface has slightly more margin for error. He will never attempt shots to difficult pin positions.

Heavy, wet rough will pull at the blade of his iron, so with a more lofted iron he plays the ball into a position which may be short of the green but which will open up the target for the next stroke.

As a plus, there are advantages to be found even in dreadful rain. The greens will saturate and this means the ball will hold quickly. This allows the player to pitch his ball right up to the flag, knowing it will stop very quickly. Putts may be hit much more firmly at the hole with much less borrowing than would otherwise be necessary. When things begin to look as if they are not

Below: Come rain or shine, golf remains one of the best-supported sports in the world.

all that bad after all, then the right attitude is developing.

What must be remembered in high wind conditions is that a head wind, which may turn a par four, normally reachable in two shots, into the equivalent of a three-shot par five, will be behind the player on a par five, making it reachable in two strokes instead of three, and so reducing it to the equivalent of a four. Of course, it cannot be as straightforward as in calm conditions, but the best professional gets his mind on top before the round starts.

The wind is used and never argued with. It always pays to set the ball off into crosswind, allowing it the benefit of wind behind when it is in its most vulnerable downflight. The professional does not believe in the old adage that a properly struck ball is not affected by wind, he assesses the strength and aims off the allowance.

Below: Kenny Brown making a beautifully smooth stroke with a putter.

The willingness to accept conditions and adapt to them is one of the tournament player's greatest strengths, even applying to playing from hills. His mind accepts completely that, should his ball be on an upslope, it will have a higher trajectory than would be normal for the club he chooses. Therefore, he takes extra club and allows the height to cancel out the length. In reverse, on a downhill he selects a more lofted club, knowing that the ball must travel with a lower flight, gaining extra distance.

His balance will be affected on sidehills and, once again, he does not argue but allows his swing to be altered by his change of balance, and the ball twists in the air accordingly. A ball above the level of the feet will hook, and a ball below must slice. (All of this is detailed in the section on sloping lies.)

Part two: the physical command

Because very successful tournament professionals all appear to swing differently it would be understandable to believe that there is no set way of swinging the club. This is not the case, for the majority of those players set out with an accepted formula in mind which they adapt accordingly. Changes are made to suit their own particular physical and temperamental requirements. There is a formula and a procedure that the world's best players go through every time they line-up to a ball and play a full shot.

Take away the various little differences and idiosyncracies and there is a definite pattern, a set of physical facts which are completed in a certain order. What they do that is different is discarded in the search for the orthodox pattern on which golf teachers base their instruction; it is what they all do the same that matters, and golf's descriptive language is based on the positions adopted.

The information given in Chapter 4 (The perfect swing) is based on the knowledge which is examined on the toughest testing-ground in the golf world, the professional golf circuit, and explained so that beginners or experienced golfers may build and understand a golf swing.

Grip and clubface

The hands of the tournament player are gripped on to the handle so that, though each performs its own function, they complement each other. The grip used is the Vardon which, with the odd exception of the little finger of the right hand sometimes overlapping (the official version), sometimes interlocking with the forefinger of the left hand, is accepted worldwide. The palms of the hands are parallel and are placed so that the back of the left hand is in line with the leading edge of the clubface.

Opposite (top): The tournament professional experiences little difficulty when playing from sloping lies. He adjusts his balance to lean with the slope rather than lean against it.

Opposite (below): Once the left hand is positioned on the grip, take up a finger grip with the right hand; professionals lay great stress on the 'feel' that this permits.

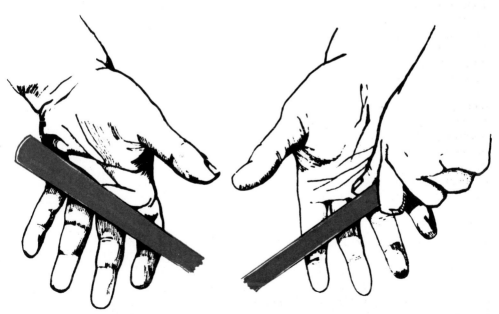

Ball position and line-up

The tournament professional prefers to position the ball opposite the inside of his left foot for all strokes, simply narrowing the width of the stance as the club in use gets shorter. There are some who prefer the method which is more suited to amateur golfers with higher handicaps, where the ball position comes back a little as the stance narrows and the club shortens. However, from the professional we learn that the ball is always forward of a point opposite the centre of the feet. No normal full shot is played from behind that point.

Whatever the choice of ball position, it is teamed up with a method of lining-up which makes for consistent accuracy. The hands introduce the leading edge of the club in a combined movement, with the right foot going forward into position. As they do so, they establish the

Below: The ball and feet position preferred by many tournament players.

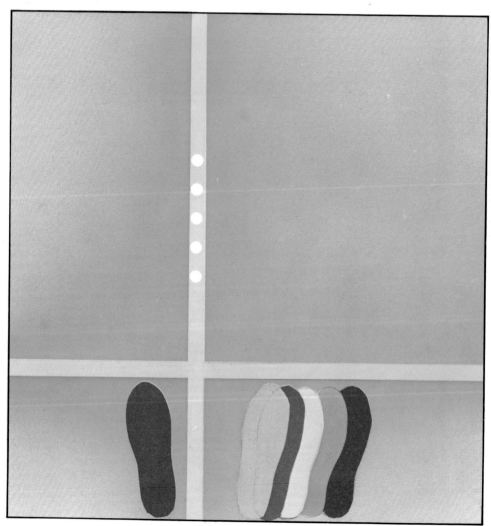

right angle to the target line, which is much easier to visualize when the left side of the body is still open (to the left) of that line. Then, with continual reference to the target, the left side of the body and the left foot are brought into line. Having the shoulders directly in line with the target is important, for the swing path of the club relies on the shoulder line for its direction.

Swing posture

The professional always positions himself to achieve balance, freedom of movement and graceful transfer of weight. This will allow a club to be delivered through a ball in an athletic movement.

The introduction of the right foot and the club to the ball creates the first movement towards good posture, bringing the shoulders forward and making the body lean forward from the waist up.

When the left side is brought forward into line, the hands and arms are lowered naturally so that they are in line with the left thigh and, in the case of a driver, about 4 inches from it.

Last, but not least, the legs flex and the toes take up their natural line (the right angle the right foot adopted in the line-up will only remain in that position if it is placed the way the player's foot would naturally be). The weight is shared evenly between both feet and towards the balls of the feet.

The shoulders should be in line above the toes, with the knees above the shoe laces. The notion which used to be claimed that the player's weight be on his heels has been completely dispelled by today's players.

The swing

There used to be a concept of backswinging where the player's first movement was to extend the club away from the ball all in one piece. Then, at a point about hip height, a wrist cock was introduced to bring the club into a position of power. This went against the body's natural inclinations, since it is almost automatic to complete this action in one movement, rather than in two distinct stages. Besides, two directions going back would surely require the same on the return journey and this made timing very difficult and was responsible for bad strokes.

The tournament professional has eliminated this faulty method, replacing it with the direct **in plane spiral** we see today. The advantage of the preparation being done this way brings a greater sense of co-ordination where the wrist cock starts as the club leaves the ball and is completed just as the arms have fully wound the shoulders. The several feet of the smooth journey of the clubhead takes exactly the same time as the few inches covered by the shoulder turn, which is exactly the time it takes the left heel to get one inch from

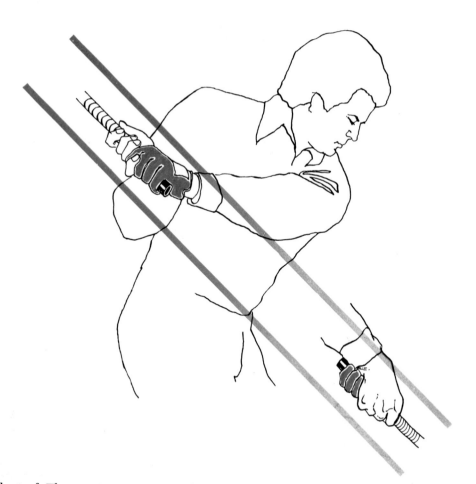

the turf. The movement is one! The feeling is one! The backswing no longer goes from the ball all in one piece, it goes all the way to the top in one movement!

In plane

There is no power to match a club delivered from a perfect plane, and although there are odd exceptions where some professionals wander off plane in the backswing, they all get back on to it for the downswing. That is why the best professional swinger is the one whose backswing spirals him directly in plane, saving himself the need for a search on the way down.

The backswing spiral

The part of the body with the longest journey to make goes first and that with the shortest last, exactly as one would expect in a spiral, which describes the movement of the backswing. As the professional's hands motivate the clubhead, they do so by engaging the wrist joints and those in turn bring the arms into action. As his wrists work they show, at any one stage, the same area of knuckle joint as at his set-up, and the arc only moves in

Above: The 'plane' is the angle on which the arc circles the body, dictated by the physique of the player and the club being used. That is why Gary Player and Lee Trevino swing flat, and taller players like Johnny Miller swing more upright.

the straightforward direction of correct plane.

His arms in turn bring the left side of the body to the front through the direct pull of the left arm winding the left shoulder from the target line. Turn is only felt in the left shoulder and never in the right, since the angle of plane requires that the right elbow and shoulder should adopt a relaxed movement.

Hips, legs and feet are drawn into the back movement as the upper body is turning away. However, to introduce them early in the movement would undermine the whole concept of a spiral and no power would be achieved from such action. The posture had the legs flexed and the right leg, although tensed by the pressure of the spiral taking place above, must attempt to retain its position. The left leg moves inwards towards the right but obviously forward of it as the hips are being turned by the spiral. The left heel leaves the ground in order to keep the hip turn level.

The downswing

Even those professionals who chose a variation in their backswing are united by the first movement of the downswing where everything must pull together. All the looseness disappears and the apparent relaxation of

Below: From the perfect 'set up', the start of the backswing spiral.

the backswing is immediately changed to trenchant attack. Backswings which are allowed, by different wrist actions, to go out of plane are drawn into a direct swingpath for the ball.

There is always argument about exactly which part of the body starts the downswing movement although it is accepted that it is the lower half, but whatever the personal feelings of each individual as to which of their muscles starts the process, there is unanimous opinion on those which do not. The hands and wrists do not undo their angle, for all of the power in that angle would be spent before the club reached the ball. The shoulders would never return before the hips for this would bring the club across the ball, eliminating the essential transfer of weight. There must be no lateral movement of the head, for a central position creates, as it holds, an invisible barrier which helps the leading edge of the clubface to return to square through the ball.

The tournament professional is aware of what these incorrect movements produce but never looks for the negative 'I mustn't do this'. He knows how he starts, and for him that is the end of it. Higher handicap players

Below: The backswing continues, the hands and arms lifting the club and winding the top of the body from the bottom to arrive at the top of the fully wound backswing.

who, because of the tension of stretched muscles caused by a poor backswing, or because of the urgency required to get back down and hit the ball, or because of anxiety to see what direction it has gone, tend to undo the swing from the top. They would certainly do better to learn that a lateral movement from the left hip is the first movement of the downswing.

Into the base of the arc

The hitting area, as it is often called, gives the impression that a swing should be delivered to a given point and then the hands unleash a mighty thrash at the ball. Fortunately, this attitude is gone from golf and the professional has proved that the swing is *through* the ball and not *to* the ball. The simpler golf swing of the player of today has removed from golf the complex hand action which necessitated a finely timed delivery of the clubhead to the ball, hoping to get the leading edge straight just at the point of maximum acceleration. Now top players swing on through the ball, safe in the knowledge that the backswing which keeps the clubhead movement simple requires a much less complicated process of adjusting. Centrifugal throw combined with a good

Below: The process then reverses, led by the lower half of the body.

wide arc and a transfer of bodyweight are sufficient, and together have removed the need for flicking and thrashing at the ball.

'Ball then turf' is another expression which is often misinterpreted. When the expert strikes an iron stroke from the turf, the contact is made with the ball by the blade as much as an inch before the blade enters the turf. Many golfers ruin not only their chances of a good stroke, but in some cases their golf swing by believing this requires a special skill. It does not!

The tournament player lines up to the ball, positioning it opposite the point he considers the stationary base of his arc. It is the lateral movement of his bodyweight and enthusiasm to swing through to the finish that results in a new base.

The throughswing

The stage of the golf swing known as the throughswing, which takes place immediately after the contact with the ball, is where the tournament professional shows no tension or anxiety, whereas the high handicap amateur often conveys a complete lack of conviction. However, much of the effectiveness of the throughswing of the professional is the result of his clubhead releasing at

Below: The action continues smoothly into the hitting area, where the iron club connects with the ball, then the turf and carries on firmly through – the player's weight at this point in the stroke carried on the left hip and leg.

122

the correct time. He knows that the moment the line of the left arm is passed by the line of the shaft the power of the wrists in the backswing is spent! The professional's successful journey down has preserved this uncocking and it takes place through and after the connection of the ball. He is often described as 'extending through the ball' – he is not! He is completing his arc. There is no conscious extension of the swing as is often believed. The arc continues on in plane and so remains in the correct curve around the player.

The finish

The finish is, by definition, the end of the swing and is often referred to in golf language as the **follow-through position**. The tournament professional makes this an established part of his action and whilst sometimes in an anxious moment he gives it up, he certainly never does so when practising. Gary Player hits thousands of balls on a practice ground, often maintaining his follow-through position until the ball actually returns to the ground. Yet he is renowned when competing for walking after his ball almost before he reaches his finish.

A correctly finished swing may be looked at in two ways. In its style and balance it could be described as the result of all that has gone before, the proof that every position in the set-up, all of the preparations in the backswing, the downswing and the throughswing were conducted properly. The tournament professional looks at it the other way. It is the home of the swing! It is what all of the other parts are built for, it is the carrot in front of the donkey! There is no better feeling for him on that last tee when the pressure is at its greatest than the knowledge that he has a sound clear memory from thousands of practice strokes just how the finish will feel, and even in a panic that memory will take his swing safely home!

The completed finish has the entire bodyweight through on to the left hip and leg, although the head is positioned directly above the point which was the base of the arc. A tournament player, by keeping his head over the ball and allowing his face to turn and face the target, allows the flow of the arc to continue in plane. He never attempts to leave his head in what used to be called the head down position where the player attempted to look at the turf long after the ball had gone. The result of this was that the right hand was forced to close over the left prematurely, forcing the plane to be broken, and also the transfer of weight was impeded.

The spinal tilt of the set-up remains throughout the backswing, is there through the ball and is the key to a balanced finish.

To be sure of the destination makes planning a journey so much simpler!

Below: The player completes the stroke in a perfectly balanced position, the plane of the swing still evident in the slope of the spine.

Making backspin pitch shots

The authority with which the tournament professional swings the club and strikes through the ball creates the tremendous backspin which he imparts. When his iron blade meets the ball it is travelling crisply forward and slightly downward, and the ball reacts to the loft of the club by immediately rotating backwards as though trying to climb up the lines on the face. This causes it to soar, and when it drops on to the green it stops immediately, and on some occasions spins back towards the player.

Many amateur players are quite capable of producing spin on their longer iron strokes where there is clubhead speed through the ball, but they cannot always emulate the professional over smaller distance strokes. In fact, amateurs usually find that the ball, even though it lands on the green, runs right on through to the back. The reason for this is that when a beginner gets to a distance which is within the range of the minimum distance iron (the wedge), they then have to play a partial swing and find it difficult to find the force which is a key contributor to backspin.

The professional uses a method which, no matter how short the distance to be covered, still requires a firm strike through the ball. With a difficult short shot to play he will always take one or two practice swings a few inches from his ball, each slightly under-powered, enough in fact to drop his ball about three-quarters of the intended journey. This adds to his authority through the actual shot, for when he lines up to the ball and has a last look at the flag, he knows he has more to do and the extra is added through the ball.

There are certain situations where backspin is not possible, even for the best of players. One of these is when the ball lies in soft, thicker grass which will get between the blade of the club and the ball at impact. Should this happen the player would happily drop the ball short of the green, allowing it to run to the flag.

Running chip shots

In normal dry conditions when a ball lies within close proximity of the putting green, the professional will prefer to keep it close to the ground, provided the first bounce is on the even surface of the green. He will choose a club which allows him minimum loft to the safety of the green's surface, with the balance of the journey to be spent rolling.

The rhythm normally associated with golf, where the wrists work and the feet work, does not come into this part of the game – in fact, action is taken to see that it does not. Movement creates backspin and that is the last thing required in the stroke. The hands, which are down the grip, are placed forward, causing the shaft to appear

to lean, with the blade of the club closed down (de-lofted so that a No. 7 iron looks like a No. 6). Through the stroke, which is played at one speed, the professional maintains his hands and wrists ahead, the angle of the shaft remaining constant. The body is kept quite still and the weight, which is slightly on the left leg in a very narrow stance, remains there throughout.

The effect on the ball is a low trajectory from the blade due to its de-lofting; the very slight backspin from what loft there is will be checked immediately on contact with the green.

Below: The forward position of the wrists when addressing the ball, if maintained throughout a chip shot, will drive a forward spin on to the ball.

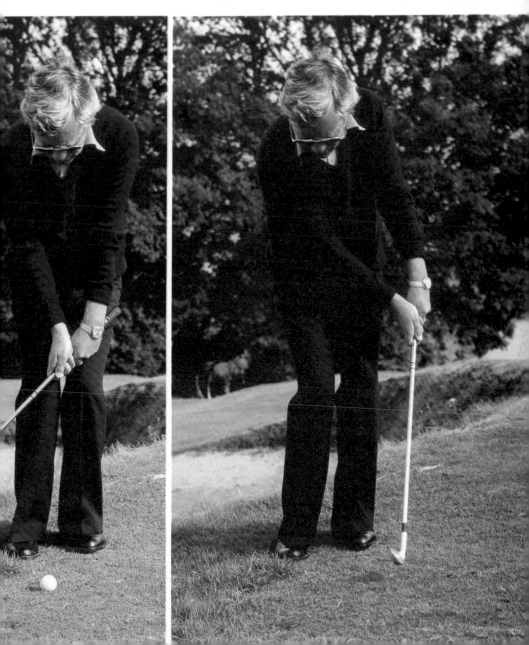

Putting

Though putting is very much a part of the mental side of golf there is much to be learned from the tournament professional. There are some who are fantastic putters and some who are average. The difference is in their confidence. There is no part of golf where so many professionals, through copying, have adopted near identical postures and movements as in putting.

In the search for a putting stroke which will have the ball rolling smoothly very soon after it leaves the blade, the putter's head is swept back and forth, very low to the ground at an even pace so that there is little impression of rapping the ball. A reverse of golf's conventional overlap grip is preferred, with the forefinger of the left hand covering the little finger of the right, and with both thumbs being placed directly on top of the handle. This minimizes movement in the wrist joints. The putter handle passes up through the centre of the palms giving the required dulling effect, unlike an active finger grip. To allow this to happen, the professional uses a putter with a very upright shaft. He positions his body well over the ball so that his eyes look directly down on the target line which the putter head moves directly along, back from the ball and forward via it towards the target. By getting his shoulders directly parallel to the line a feeling of squareness makes a straight roll simpler. Unlike the shoulders, the feet may aim wherever comfortable being still, they have no effect on the action. It is variation here which is seen by amateurs as the reason for believing putting cannot be taught.

One thing that the tournament professional does is seek, and receive, help from his fellows. There is no part of the game where advice and help is sought more than with the putter.

Left: Tony Jacklin of England, former winner of both the British and United States Open Championships, blames much of his loss of form in recent years on the desertion of his putting touch. However, here is one which did not get away.
Opposite: Gary Player takes great care before putting, but once over the ball gives it a firm rap.

Part three: control of the ball

The galleries gasp in amazement at the sight of the tournament player bending the ball around an obstacle when, in fact, it is much simpler than a straight shot. Most top professionals steer clear of ever making a dead-straight flight, particularly when using the longer clubs, preferring to spin the ball either with a **fade-spin** (left to right) or as a **draw-spin** (right to left). Shorter irons, with the extra control given by their backspin are often the only shots many competitors hit straight.

The problem of a straight flight is that, under pressure, a player can cause a ball to veer away to the right or to the left. A ball played with a deliberate 'shape' on it may, under similar circumstances, spin a bit farther off course than intended, but then it will be in the direction of the player's choice and he will have already studied the hazards and problems which exist on that particular side of the fairway.

The preference of the bigger man is to fade the ball which, although having the effect of a slight loss of power, is closely allied to backspin and has greater control. A ball flying with fade-spin will run very little on landing, and this is a great advantage when playing a long stroke on to a green. Smaller players, particularly if they are less physically strong, prefer the draw-flight, right to left, for it is assisted by overspin. When a drawn ball hits the ground it runs on and on, making up for the yardage physical strength sometimes precludes.

It is fairly simple to understand how the slight spin of the two shapes is created. Fade is a mild form of slice, where the clubface is moved across the ball from out to in whilst remaining slightly open. Draw is from an in to out arc, with the clubface just closing. Common sense suggests that the higher plane of a tall man's swing would suit the fade shot, travelling down on the ball from upright. The small man's shallower plane would naturally come from in to out and a draw should be much simpler. However, control is not always a case of common sense. Personal preference is important, and one sees small men like Lee Trevino fading his shots and tall ones, such as Greg Norman, drawing his. Nevertheless, they are exceptions to the general rule.

What the reader should realize is that the movements which the tournament professional makes to create the various controlled spins are dictated entirely by feel. He pictures in his mind the flight he wishes to make, transmits that to the related feel of hands and club, as to how they will work into, or across, the ball and from that flow the directions and plane of his swing. He does not, as many amateurs believe, do the opposite, which is to direct the swing into certain positions which would cause spin. Whilst the two may appear to achieve the

Opposite: The advantage of a fade (a mild, deliberate slice of the ball) on the flight of iron shots, is that the ball will stop as it lands on the green. A draw shot (a mild hook) carries a bit of overspin and is inclined to run on landing. Many professionals use fade with irons and draw with woods, gaining the best of both worlds.

same end, this rarely happens. The slight variations of the professionals come from the mildest of adjustments which gain their subtlety from that magic word in golf — feel!

Fading the ball

The feel of sliding the clubface slightly across the ball requires the professional to position the ball forward in the stance, and in doing so he makes his shoulders turn open to the left of the target. His impression when swinging through the ball is that the clubface is not going to close, but remain very slightly open.

The result is that, as the shoulders dictate an out to in swing path, which the club swings along in search of the forward ball position, the hips must turn away before contact is made. The clubface must drag across the ball; the sidespin is then assured.

Drawing the ball

The feeling the professional has in the drawn shot is that he is going to bring the clubface up into the ball against the resistance of the left side of his body, and he brings the ball back in the stance. His shoulders squared up, even close up, will be in line with a point to the right of the desired target. They define the swing path as in to out and the clubface closes up in search of the actual target, creating the overspin of an in to out arc.

Height of flight

Apart from choosing to fly the ball left or right, the professional has two other choices, high and low. Many years ago it was believed that a low ball travelled farther and drivers were designed with hardly any loft on the face. Today's clubs have plenty of angle, for it is accepted that a ball flying high flies farther. However, into strong winds, or under branches of trees a low ball is often required and the professional, once again by feel, applies movement to produce heights of flight.

High ball

The more creative and active the body movements in the swing, the higher the ball flies. In a search for this creative feel, when lining-up, the professional lowers his hands towards his knees and produces a very early wrist action upwards, out of plane in the backswing. His stance narrows, making the feet and ankles work. The ball is positioned forward, which helps clear his left side out of the path of the club on the throughswing, and up goes the ball!

Low ball

Into the teeth of a gale the last thing the professional wishes to do is to impart backspin. There are two methods employed to keep the ball down in flight, one requiring great skill, the other much simpler.

The first method has the ball positioned well back in the stance and the player addresses it with his hands well forward. This combination shuts down the loft of the club so that the trajectory is very low. The blow is delivered as a punch down on the ball. Many professionals dislike this technique for it conflicts with their instinctive forward ball position and is inclined to lead the backswing very quickly inside a movement which promotes hooking.

The simpler version is to choose a longer club, which would normally travel more distance than that required. Then, by holding it lower down the handle, which stifles the wrist action, and by widening the stance, which stifles the leg work, the ball is driven forward into a low flight. The dullness of the movements quietens the spin and the ball does not soar.

Part four: the clubs for the job

Many professionals carry two fairway woods in their set which in fact send the ball the same distance. One, however, may have its clubface turned slightly outwards and make the ball fade in flight. The other may have the opposite characteristic and send the ball in a draw. It may not be as obvious as that, even to the player himself. Perhaps it is not the club design but merely the fact that he has found a club which always sends the ball a certain direction. This makes him happy, for when he plays a hole with trouble on one side he will use the club which always compensates by sending the ball the other way. At the other end of the scale, he will probably also carry more than one wedge – often choosing one which flies the ball lower than usual, and another which lifts the ball higher.

The tournament professional never adapts himself to suit his clubs, but always the clubs to suit him, and when he comes across a club he dislikes he simply discards it. It is perfectly normal to see his matched set consisting only of the No. 2 iron to the No. 9 iron. His woods are very often favourite individuals, as are his wedge, sand iron and putter.

The matching of the irons is essential because with their matched swing weight and regular difference of loft, he can tell exactly how many yards difference there is in the carry of each. Knowing this, choosing the right club becomes much simpler, particularly when yardages are charted for him at most events. Every golfer should find out how far he sends the ball. By hitting 20 or 30 balls with one club in calm conditions, then pacing to the average, a guide figure is established. It is merely a question of adding or subtracting approximately 10 yards per club. Even the least competitive golfer should know the approximate yardage of his tee shots. Then, by subtracting from the measurements always given on the scorecard, a fairly accurate choice of club may be made.

Part five: playing different types of courses

Modern jet travel has so reduced the size of the world that it is almost possible for the tournament professional to play competitively somewhere for 52 weeks of the year. As a result, he has to be able to adapt his game to suit entirely different conditions almost overnight. There are types of shots which can only be played on certain types of courses and some of these are given here for the benefit of the reader whose golf may occasionally take him a little way away from home. After all, the character of a golf course is dependent on its subsoil and that can vary within only a few miles, particularly in an island country.

Links courses

Most professionals, whilst they enjoy the traditions of playing on seaside links, which in Britain is always the home of the Open Championship, tend to dislike links courses. This is born out of distrust, for they are never quite sure what the next bounce is going to do. The sandy soil quickly drains water away from the putting greens and makes them unpredictable. Often a good shot played directly on to a green will bounce off, its backspin having no effect whatsoever. Apart from this, most links are very old and the humps and hollows which used to be out of range when the courses were laid out, seem to now be just where modern swings, using modern equipment, put the ball. As if this were not enough, there always seems to be a gale blowing!

The prime piece of advice for these courses is to stay away from lofted clubs. There is no point in tossing a high shot up on to a links green; far better to master the run-up. This is the stroke explained in Chapter 5, except that the first bounce does not have to be on the putting

Below: St Andrews, the traditional home of the sport.

surface; indeed, it may be many yards short of it and it may have to take into account borrows created by sidehills of sand dunes. One good thing about the short, tight grass of a links course is that it is predictable, and a ball will run across it. On many occasions the professional will use a putter and hug the ground all the way.

On the longer strokes with the ball lying so tight, greater accuracy is required, and a wooden club catching the ground short of the ball may well bounce and cause a topped shot. The professional often uses a more lofted wood and, by putting the ball farther back in his stance, gets his hands forward of it at address. This technique is often used with irons, too, and it causes a downward blow on the ball, described as squeezing (with a wood), and punching (with an iron).

The point from which he plays his shot to the harder greens is obviously more important, and yardage is readily sacrificed for the benefit of position. When there is no chance of carrying a greenside bunker and staying on the green with the second shot, it is the opening at the front of the green which must be the objective when positioning the tee shot.

With the wind blowing hard against him, the professional accepts that some of the par four holes will be out of reach in two strokes. He never forces his swing when going into wind for this would damage his play and could cause a loss of control. His policy is to accept a stroke dropped, bearing in mind that a headwind going out, will be a tail wind coming in!

Any reader who has not experienced a fiery seaside putting green has a shock in store, for the tight grass which grows on sand is bleached by sun and wind, and a first visit unfortunately produces more three putts than twos. The professional often carries a spare, very light-headed putter – on these greens the ball must be rolled by a gentle stroke, never rapped.

Because of the cunning placing of guarding bunkers, plus the fact that the ball will not stop if flown over them, the professional often has to play well away from the flag to be on the green at all. On such occasions he is delighted to get down in two putts and makes no real effort to hole out the first, merely rolling it into a position which will make the next one easy.

The key to seaside approach putting and, indeed, to approach chips, is to make sure that the piece left is never downhill! On a windy day, and on a fast green, holing-out from 6 or 7 feet uphill is much simpler than from as little as 2 feet going downhill.

The professional is often seen walking a long distance to stand by the hole before playing a stroke, just to see which side of it would be best to finish on so as to have that next putt uphill!

Overleaf: The famous ninth tee at Turnberry, Scotland.

Inland courses

The majority of inland golf courses are parkland, which means they are constructed on soil which either was, or could have been, used for agricultural purposes. The others are made up of what are known as heath or forest courses. There are some which are a mixture of all three, indeed, the fine new Duke and Duchess Courses built on the Duke of Bedford's estate are laid out in a forest in the centre of agricultural land, and yet have many of the characteristics of a links course. For example, the sub-soil is purely sand, being on a strip of that geological layer which runs across Bedfordshire and Buckinghamshire.

On heath or forest courses many of the seaside strokes have to be played, for their exceptional drainage makes the turf tight and fast running, but on the parkland courses a much more straightforward game of golf may be played.

There is great reward for the better striker of the ball who knows that a good high iron shot will, when it thumps into the green, stay there! Tournament players much prefer this type of golf where much less is left to chance.

A tee shot landing will find the turf softer, and there is less chance of it kicking off at a weird angle, so the player is encouraged to hit fully through. Even if he does send the ball a little off line the punishment for being badly positioned on this type of course is nothing like as severe as on a links, for with softer and more holding greens he can fly over guarding bunkers knowing that the ball will stop quickly.

Fairway shots are easier, too, for the ball sits up, often so high that a driver can be used from the grass. This, of course, should never be attempted by higher handicap players but should give them encouragement to have a free swing with a No. 3 wood. Even if a little inaccurate, the cushion of grass under the ball on parkland courses gives a little margin for error.

The professional knows that the more positive his strike through an iron the greater the backspin, and his aggressive through-the-ball stroke often results in large pieces of turf coming out after the ball (which should be carefully replaced by his or her caddy). Turf should never be confused with divot, for turf comes from a clubhead which has already contacted the ball and is accelerating on through after it. Many club golfers who attempt to follow this example promote the clubhead early to the ball by undoing their hand action too soon with the result that the blade meets the ground before the ball, and the divot rises between clubface and ball. The lesson to be learned is that the professional attacks through the ball, and never to the ball.

Around the green, the professional virtually discards the chip and run shot as played with a straight-faced club like a No. 6 or No. 7. He does occasionally make a little shot which shoots forward, but does this with his wedge, sometimes even his sand iron. The softer grass of the inland fairway allows him the scope of various flights from these lofted irons, when there is less chance of the flange of the club bouncing. Controlling the height of the flight and the run-out of the ball is governed by the amount his hands are placed forward of the blade. This can vary from a distinct lean forwards of several inches to being virtually directly above the clubhead.

There are many inland courses with putting greens as fast, and as difficult, as links courses. Augusta National, home of the United States Masters, has magnificent but frighteningly fast surfaces, and by means of television satellites golfers the world over have seen dreams and nightmares come true. The slick surfaces of Walton Heath in England are matched by those of Spain's Costa Del Sol courses, which though close to the sea are nevertheless inland by design and nature.

However, the greens of average inland courses are only about half as fast as those mentioned above, and players who play all their golf on them never acquire the touch of those who learned and play on a slippery surface. It is possible to hit the ball into the hole, and a professional can do just that; should he miss, the return will not be too long. Of course, like anyone else, he prefers putting directly up a slope. So, if the hole is on a tricky part of the green, he will study exactly which side is best to finish on when approaching.

Part six: playing the designer

Although professionals are capable of drives of fiersome length, they only unleash them when circumstances warrant. They know from experience that the odd burst of bad temper arising from a bad finish on the previous hole usually results in two bad holes! They will, therefore, play many positional strokes during a round. They do this out of an appreciation of the designer, and what he had in mind. Readers should also attempt this, and before 'bashing' off should take a moment to stand on the teeing ground and work out what the architect did, and why.

Dog-leg holes

The professional knows that when a hole **dog-legs**, which means it turns a corner, a good architect will have done two things. Firstly, he will have placed an obstacle on the corner to confound those who think they can short-cut over it. Secondly, he will have placed trouble, normally a guarding bunker, in front of the green on the opposite side. Therefore, the professional has the choice of either playing safely away from the corner and facing a difficult second, or of incurring a greater risk by skirting the trouble on that corner to make the second stroke easier.

To the high handicap golfer there is a much more simple solution, for he will more likely than not have a handicap stroke on such a difficult hole. By playing a No. 3 wood he can remain short of the problems on the corner. Then, by hitting a lofted wood or a long iron over the trouble, away from that guarding bunker, he is left with a simple pitch on to the green from the open side.

Out-of-bounds

When there is an out-of-bounds along one side (say, for example, the right) the professional will tee off either by applying a bit of hook spin, or by using that wooden club he carries which never slices, leaving the driver in the bag. The club golfer, who is prone to slicing anyway, when under pressure after a failure to complete a good turn, should be satisfied to tee off with a lofted wood, the additional backspin minimizing the chance of slice spin. There is no point in hoping that it just might not slice this time, because it will!

Tiered greens

If a professional is not quite sure of the correct club required for the stroke to a tiered green, he will always choose a shorter one, and hit firmly. The last thing a golfer should do there is to overclub for should his ball arrive on a level above that where the pin is, he is subsequently likely to incur three putts from a difficult downhill.

Fairway bunkers

Before playing from the fairway bunker the professional studies the lie of the land and picks the best spot for the next stroke. From bitter experience he knows that attempts to carry a ball all the way to the green flounder dismally, due to only the slightest early contact with the sand, and attempting to pick a ball off the top very seldom succeeds.

Water hazards

When playing to a pin tucked close behind a bunker, the professional can take a bit of a risk. After all, if he falls short, his ability with a sand iron may still salvage par. However, water is a different proposition which demands more respect. A cunning designer who places a lake in front of the green will have a pin position very close to the water, and water has a penalty stroke as a reward for those who try to be too clever. It is best therefore to play to a point beyond the pin and accept a longer return putt. To drop with a plop is a wasted stroke to which is added a penalty shot!

Opposite: Occasionally, a player who always draws the ball fails to do so – as happened here to Fuzzy Zoeller, United States Masters Champion. His ball ended up against the spectator barrier, leaving him no choice but to wait patiently for a ruling from a PGA official – in this case, Tony Grey of the European Tournament Division.

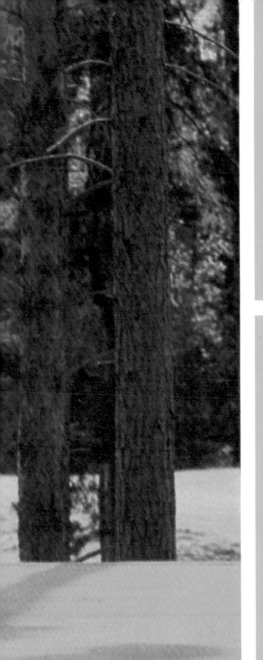

CHAPTER 7

FORMS
OF PLAY

Golf is one of the few sports which someone can play on their own – competing against the par of the course. Nevertheless, it is a game which should, whenever possible, be played and enjoyed in the company of 'real' opponents – whether in singles matchplay, fourball matchplay or strokeplay.

Golf is one of the few games which can be played alone, and an individual can play a medal match or stroke match against the par of the course, complete a score, subtract his handicap and so determine who won! It can also be determined on a match-play basis, where by deducting the handicap stroke at the appropriate hole an up or down result is obtained. However, the friendly tradition of golf has strived to bring people together, and the handicap system which has made all men equal requires that golfers play together in pairs at least. Pairs, in any case, have priority over single golfers on the course, and the lone player is required to make way for accepted pairs, trios or fours – which is the maximum number in a match.

Match play

Match play was the original form of play, probably because the totally unplayable positions a ball could get into in those days would have made the completion of a whole course almost an impossibility. Matches were therefore decided on a hole-by-hole result. Match play is played either as a singles, which is one golfer against an opponent; or in a foursome, which is the ball shared in an alternate shot pattern between two golfers, matched against that of two opponents. Although strokes are played alternately during the hole, each hole is started in a strict order so that one player tees off on all the odd numbered holes and the partner takes the evens. Finally, it is played as a four-ball, better-ball match, when both pairs all play a ball and the better score made by any player in one team is matched against that of the opposing side.

In match play, the handicap differences are taken, as dictated by the stroke index of the course, and printed for all to see on the scorecard – on the completion of each hole.

Stroke play

Stroke play is a much simpler form which allows a player, playing either as a pair, as a three-ball, or as a four-ball, to compete against many others playing on the course that day. The opponents are called partners, and each player is required to complete the recording of the score made at each hole by his partner.

An additional column is provided on the score card for the player to keep a record of his own for reference at the completion of the round.

The strokes deducted as handicap are taken from the total on completion. In the four-ball, better-ball, the best score of the pair is recorded, with the handicap deducted on a hole-by-hole basis, as though in match play.

Stableford

This is a system of scoring which can be a more pleasant way of competing for higher handicap golfers simply because it allows for the odd disastrous hole.

Two points are awarded to the player who scores a par figure, after the deduction of the applicable handicap allowance, on a hole-by-hole basis. Should the net score on the hole be one better than par, three points are awarded. Two better would receive four points, and so on. On the other hand, if one over par is the result then only one point is the award and more than one over would receive no points at all. This means the player need not complete a very bad hole, but pick up and carry on to the next, so saving time from being wasted and his colleagues' patience from being tested!

Stableford has certainly taken over from a form of play which was, and indeed still is in Britain, called a bogey competition, and in other countries, a par competition. This was originally intended for the lone golfer to compete against the par (bogey used to describe par in Britain, but the American version of the word is now accepted worldwide and means one over par) of the course as a means of competition to stop him feeling isolated. As a competition, which it later became for many players, it was totally unfair. A player scoring a two-under-par eagle on a hole was no better than an opponent who scored a one-under birdie – both were one up. At the other extreme, a player who just dropped one stroke on a very difficult long par four would go one down – as would one who might have had three shots out of bounds and a couple in the lake, and then retired.

The different approach to match play and stroke play

Golfers, naturally, feel differently about straightforward matches played by two people on a hole-by-hole basis, and the completing of 18 holes where the best total wins over many competitors. In match play it is essential that a golfer plays intelligently according to the tactics and position of his opponent. For example, should the opponent put his tee shot on a difficult hole out of bounds, requiring him to add two strokes to the total, it would be commendable for the other golfer to play conservatively down the fairway, even using an iron to be safe. It would be unwise to follow the leader, and go out of bounds too! Should an opponent have taken so many strokes that the player need only take two putts to win, there is no point in attacking the hole with a first putt, when a safe lay-up will do. Foolish risks taken when being up (the term used to describe the amount of holes won, more than lost, in a match) only result in seeing the lead slip away.

On the other hand, when trailing, a player must often take chances. It is pointless playing a careful approach to the centre of the 18th green if the opponent is already by the flag and one up. It may be essential to attempt a difficult carry when all appears to be lost. It is a case of playing the man and not the course.

Stroke play

This is the test of the complete golfer for it shows up all the flaws in the temperament, and proves the player's ability to think well. A good score is achieved when all the holes which are played well are teamed with common sense on those where something goes wrong. The best stroke players accept that things do go wrong, even on the best days!

On all holes, to think one shot ahead is essential, and placing the ball so that the next shot is made easier makes those good holes come more often. However, when in trouble, one must accept what has gone and keep a cool defensive head. To attempt to carry vast journeys from a bad lie when trying to make up, by using a club with insufficient loft, is the cause of most spoiled cards. It is better to hit a lofted iron to the spot, which might benefit the next stroke.

What a partner is doing should be kept in perspective, for golf is a great leveller, and although the partner seems many strokes ahead, one bad hole can often reverse the whole situation. There is, of course, a time to attack as well as to defend. Looking at a wide open fairway from a tee is a good moment. When a flag is at the back of the green, with the guarding bunkers all at the front, is another. An uphill putt with little or no borrow is perfect.

To recognize the difference between defence and attack in advance, rather than in hindsight, is the strength of the stroke player!

The international game

For more than a century, professional golfers have left the shores of Britain and, like missionaries, spread the gospel of golf across the world. They built courses, taught the game, and established the traditions of sportsmanship which go with it. Surely they could not have forseen the incredible fruits which have come from their labours.

As each nation developed, its own talented players became professional, forming associations modelled on the British PGA and soon championships and tournaments were held. In those times Britain's competitive professionals would travel abroad and pick up the titles, virtually unchallenged. Those days are gone and the wheel has turned full circle with the competitors from

Above: The magnificent course at Torrequebrada, on the outskirts of Torremolinos, home of the 1979 Spanish Open Championship.

those younger nations not only winning 'on their own patch' but coming to Britain to claim championships.

Each part of the world has developed its own full-time tournament circuit. The Americans start the year in Arizona, then proceed to California. From there they go into Florida, next to Carolina, in fact they simply follow the sun the year round to complete the most prosperous circuit there is.

The European circuit, though perhaps not favoured with so much sunshine, starts off in Portugal, then on to Spain, Italy and France, finally moving up to the colder countries as summer arrives.

The Japanese have formed their own most lucrative circuit, playing more than thirty major events whilst, not far away, the Asians play in exotic places like the Philippines, Calcutta, Kuala Lumpur and Taiwan. Many other countries, like South Africa, Australia and New Zealand have their own 'tours'.

In golf, as in some other sports, as the weather puts competition out of action in one part of the world, it sets it off in another; and that other place is only a jet flight away. So we have Australian professionals invading the Asian circuit, and South Africans, New Zealanders, Australians moving in on Europe in the spring. Eventually the 'cream' from these circuits give the 'big one' a try. The United States circuit is the fiercest competitive golf tour in the world, and many a foreigner has headed

Above: The idyllic setting and perfect golfing conditions of the course on the island of Maui, in the Hawaiian Islands.

home with his tail between his legs after fruitless years.

There are certain events played which are of great prestige and which are truly international. The Open Championships of the various nations, where overseas players, provided they qualify, flock to play, are examples, and there can be no championship in the world in any sport which attracts such an international field than the most famous of all, the British Open, drawing competitors from no less than 27 countries.

Professional golf has attracted the ladies, with the result that they have a travelling circus of their own with the entire troupe travelling the world in all-the-

year-round tournaments. Their formation of National Associations is smaller than that of the men, neverthe-less they are well and truly established.

The United States has taken the role of forerunner with its Ladies' Professional Golfers' Association, and it is on this that the groups forming in other countries are modelling themselves.

A player's card has to be earned before any girl may play on the United States Ladies Tour, and the standard is very high indeed. When the American lady players arrived in another country they, just as the British men did many years ago, dominated the events. But the wheel is turning and already Mexican, Australian, South African and Japanese girls are beginning to emerge as winners in major events.

In this incredible burgeoning of international golf, male and female, there are no variations in the rules so there is no need to be a fluent linguist. There is a code in golf, an international code based on a tradition of good sportsmanship and good fellowship the likes of which are found in no other sport. The foundations of the game were well and truly laid!

Below: Professional golf circuits have spread throughout the world, but the traditions of sportsmanship and courtesy have remained constant.

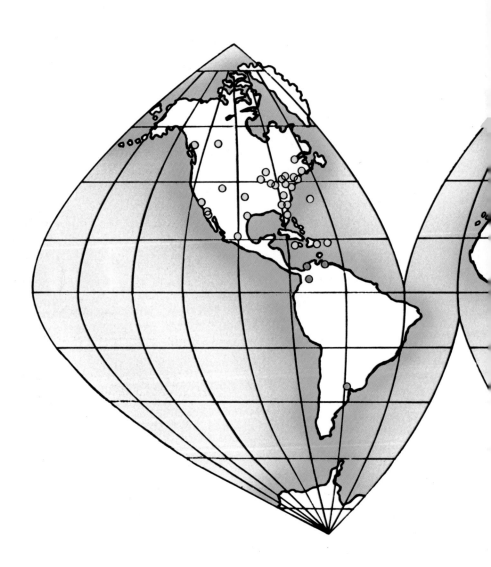

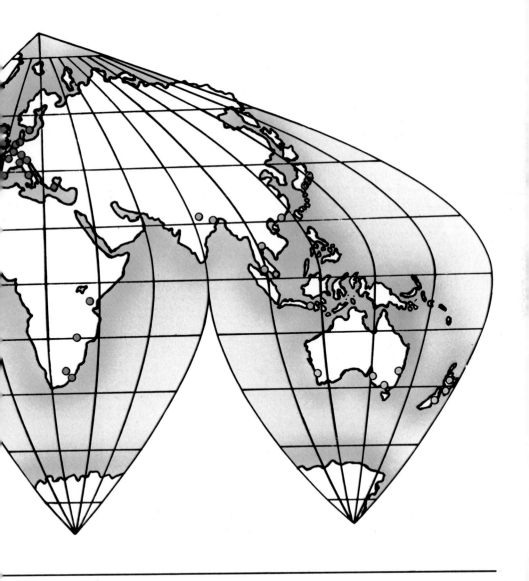

INDEX